INVENTIONS

MICHAEL HOLT

First published in Great Britain in 1990 by
Belitha Press Limited
31 Newington Green, London N16 9PU
Copyright © Belitha Press Limited and
Gareth Stevens, Inc. 1990
Illustrations/photographs copyright © in this
format by Belitha Press Limited and Gareth
Stevens, Inc. 1990
All right reserved. No part of this book may be
reproduced or utilized in any form or by any
means, electronic or mechanical, includin
photocopying, recording or by any information
storage and retrieval system, without permission
in writing from the Publisher.
ISBN 1 85561 014 0
Reprinted in 1994
Printed in China for Imago

British Library Cataloguing in Publication Data
CIP data for this book is available from the British Library

Acknowledgements

Photographic credits:

Aspect Picture Library 5, 20, 55 right
Bridgeman Art Library 8, 21 bottom, 49
Elizabeth Whiting Associates 5
Mary Evans Picture Library 6, 37, 38, 41, 43
Tim Furniss 55 bottom
Susan Griggs/Dimitri Ilic 51
Robert Harding Picture Library 44, 58
Michael Holford 15, 17 top, 21 top, 22, 25, 33
Hulton Picture Company 51
Hutchison Library 17 bottom
Mansell Collection 53 bottom
NASA 56 right, 59
Planet Earth 48
Ronan Picture Library 7, 9 bottom, 53 top, 56 left
Science Museum Library 28
Science Photo Library 9 top
Spectrum Colour Library 35, 50
Topham Picture Library

Illustrated by: Peter Gregory, Pat Fogarty, Eugene Fleury and Cathy Barrett

Series editor: Neil Champion
Educational consultant: Dr Alistair Ross
Designed by: Groom and Pickerill
Picture research and art editing: Ann Usborne

Contents

1: What are Inventions?
Inventions in Society 4
Inventions and the Inventor 6
Inventions, Patents and Sales 8

2: The Earliest Inventions
From Making Tools to Making Money 10
From Yoke to Wheel 12
Words and Numbers 14
Cities of the Ancient World 16

3: Invention on the Move
Early Transport 18
Sailing Ships 20
Finding the Way 22

4: Inventions for War
Slings and Catapults 24
Gunpowder and Cannons 26

5: The Advance of Science
Leonardo da Vinci 28
From Near and Far 30

Telling the Time 32
Water-mills and Windmills 34
From Printing to Air Pressure 36

6: The Industrial Revolution
Coal-mining and the Age of the Engine 38
The Age of Steam 40
The Spinning Industry 42
The Metal Revolution 44
The Age of Electricity 46
Revolution in Farming and Food 48
Oil and Gas 50

7: 20th Century Technology
Mass Production 52
Flight 54
Getting the Message Across 56
The Computer and the Future 58

Glossary 60
Index 62

Words found in **bold** are explained
in the glossary on pages 60 and 61

1: What are Inventions?

Inventions in Society

When you prise open a lid with a spoon or you play on a see-saw with a friend you are actually using one of the simplest and best machines ever invented. It is called the lever. With a lever you can move much heavier weights than could be managed using just muscle power. The people who built the pyramids in Egypt used levers to move the heavy blocks. ▼

Inventions are the result of someone putting material things together to make something new. All of the machines and gadgets you see in the home are inventions. What makes people invent? 'Necessity', they say, 'is the mother of invention.' Many inventions have made life easier for people to live; useless inventions die with their inventor. An invention may be the result of a happy accident but it will very likely need long painstaking work in perfecting it. Rarely does someone sit down to invent something definite. Many inventions create their own demand, such as soap, paper money, or the motor car. Before their invention no one saw the need for them.

Invention or Discovery?

Invention is not the same as discovery. Discoverers find something that has always been there but was not known of before. Inventors find a way to put it to use. For example, it was long known that steam comes out of a boiling kettle with some force. But it took an inventor like James Watt to make practical use of that force in the steam-engine.

Inventions Around You

Look around you. How many inventions can you spot? You are woken by an alarm clock in a house perhaps warmed by central heating. You listen to the radio or watch television. You go to school in a car or bus. You go to the cinema. In school you see pictures made by overhead projectors. Offices have **word processors, fax** machines and cordless telephones. Salesmen use car phones. And everywhere there is the computer.

▲ A modern kitchen contains all sorts of useful inventions. There might be a gas or electric cooker, a microwave, an electric mixer, a dishwasher, even a television and a telephone.

The computer has done much to change the way people work. ▼

WHAT ARE INVENTIONS?

Inventions and the Inventor

On 14 December 1903, at ▶ Kitty Hawk, North Carolina, the Wright Brothers made the first powered flight in their biplane, the Flyer. Wilbur flew the machine, his brother, Orville, started the engine. The plane crashed after a short flight. Wilbur was unhurt.

Who Invented What?

● Thomas Alva Edison, an American, was perhaps the greatest inventor in history. He patented more than 1,000 inventions in sixty years. He invented the electric light bulb and the gramophone (phonograph).

● Walter Hunt of New York invented the safety pin in a few hours one day in 1846. He simply twisted a length of wire into the shape we use today.

● Wilbur and Orville Wright flew their first flying machine, the Flyer, at Kitty Hawk, North Carolina, USA in 1903.

● In 1908, Ernest Swinton of Britain invented the tank, first used in World War I.

● The escalator was invented in 1900 by the Waygood Otis Elevator Company, in America.

How Do Inventors Work?

Most inventors work alone and an invention may be the brain-child of one man. Michael Faraday, for example, invented the electric motor. The same invention may be made by different inventors working independently. Joseph Henry, working in America, hit upon the same idea as Faraday in Britain. Some inventors work in teams, perhaps in **laboratories**, and pool their ideas. Television needed years of patient work by many inventors working independently.

Inventors and Scientists

Inventors rarely discover scientific laws. They try to find ways to put them to use. For instance, the Wright brothers did not discover the laws of flight: they used them to invent the first heavier-than-air flying machine, which led to the modern aeroplane. Nor did the American inventor Alexander Graham Bell discover the laws of electricity: he put them to use in inventing the telephone. The Italian Guglielmo Marconi used the laws of **electromagnetic waves** that others had worked out

and invented the radio transmitter and receiver. The English inventor C. S. Cockerell used, but did not discover, the laws of air pressure. He used them to invent the hovercraft.

Who Invented What?

- Hiram Maxim, an American-English inventor, invented the machine-gun in 1883.
- Charles Gabriel Pravaz of France invented the **hypodermic** needle and syringe in 1853.
- Henry Seely of the USA invented the electric iron in 1879.

◀ On 18 October 1892, Alexander Graham Bell inaugurated the 1520 km telephone link between New York and Chicago. Bell is seen here speaking into the mouthpiece of his own invention, the telephone.

Hovercraft ride on a cushion of air created by a curtain of high pressure air blown down around the edge of the hovercraft. The air curtain holds the cushion of air in place. ▼

WHAT ARE INVENTIONS?

Inventions, Patents and Sales

Fun and Games
- In 1893, George Ferris invented the Ferris Wheel of the fun fair.
- An American, Charles B. Darrow, invented Monopoly. He thought of it during the **depression** in the 1930s when everyone liked to imagine they had money to spend.

Bicycle Facts
- In 1887, H. J. Lawson invented a safety bicycle, that replaced the dangerous 'high-wheeler'.
- John Dunlop, a Scottish veterinary surgeon, fitted the first pneumatic (air-filled) tyres to a bicycle in 1888.
- The first variable gears were fitted to a bicycle in 1889.

The Penny Farthing bicycle, ▶ or *ordinary*, was developed in 1870. The front wheel was about 1 metre 32 cm in diameter, the top of it coming up to a man's shoulders. It had no gears. The rider perched on a saddle over the big wheel, the 'penny'. It had a rear-wheel brake.

Patenting an Invention
A patent is a government grant. It gives inventors the sole right to make and sell their inventions. It also gives them the legal right to stop anyone from copying their inventions and producing them. Inventors file all the facts about their inventions at the patents office in their country. They have to list their claims to show that the idea is new. So they must study earlier patents to make sure the idea is **original**.

Selling an Invention
Thousands of inventions are patented each year but not all of them change the world. It is one thing to patent an invention, quite another to sell it! For example, the idea of air-filled rubber tyres was patented in 1845 by R. W. Thomson. But it wasn't until 1888 that John Dunlop patented the bicycle tyre. Nobody has yet found a really practical use for bouncing putty, invented some years ago.

Very few inventors make money out of their inventions. If they are poor, they must find **backers** or borrow money to get started. Or they may license a company to sell their invention. The more unusual an invention, the

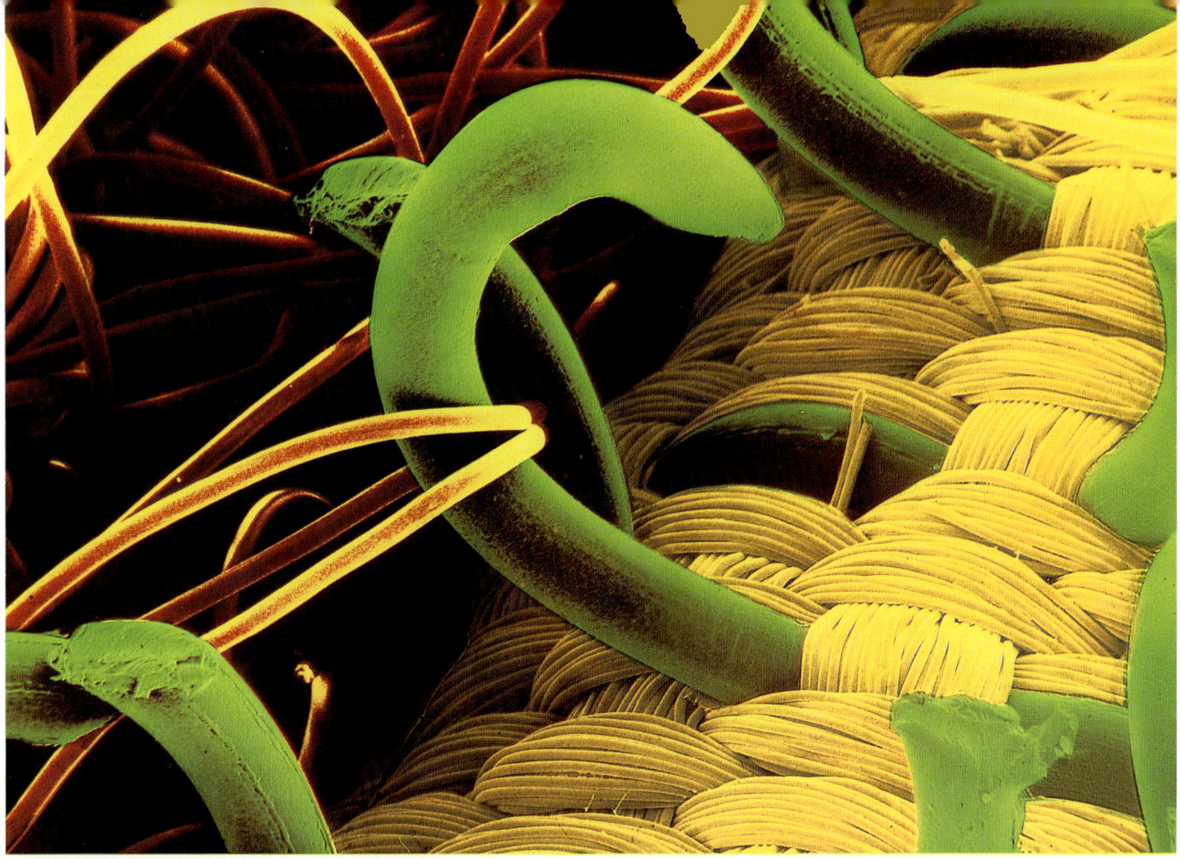

The sticky burr of the ▲ burdock plant was the inspiration for the invention of Velcro. In the 1950s Georges de Mestral, of Switzerland, saw that the burrs had tiny hooks – which attach themselves to clothing and animal fur. The hooks and loops in two pieces of Velcro fabric cling together in the same way. The photograph above shows a piece of Velcro magnified to show the hooks and loops clearly.

◀ Guglielmo Marconi (1874-1937), the Italian inventor of the wireless (radio), with one of his wireless sets on board a luxury yacht. His wireless was fitted to many ocean-going ships in the early 1900s.

harder it is to sell it. Marconi invented **wireless telegraphy** in 1894. But the radio did not become a household item until the 1920s. Inventors can make the quickest profits on small inventions that are a great improvement on things already on sale. If they are marketed well, the public will readily accept such gadgets. For instance, in 1903 King Gillette sold a mere 168 of the razor blades he had invented in 1895. They soon caught on though. The next year he sold an amazing 12 million blades.

2: THE EARLIEST INVENTIONS

From Making Tools to Making Money

Early Tool-making

About 10,000 years ago people learnt how to plant and grow crops, and so invented farming. The first farm tool was the wooden digging stick. This became a hand-held hoe with a wooden handle. The next tool was the **sickle**, shaped like a sheep's jaw. Then came stone hand-axes, fur coats, skin huts, leather bags and buckets. Later iron blades were made by beating out iron from **meteorites**. The first hunters invented the spear, sling, boomerang, **bolas**, blow-gun and dart, and the bow and arrow. From this they found how to make the spring trap.

Taming Flames

No one really knows where or when people first used fire – it may have been over a million years ago. Taming fire was something that no animal could do. People invented a way to make fire by striking flint stones together to

Cooking by Fire

After people had invented ways to make fires, they discovered how to cook meat. They invented the cooking pot. Someone probably coated a basket with thick clay and found they could boil water in it over a fire. Later someone else left out the basket and made a simple earthenware pot.

The Spring Trap

A sapling is tied to the ground and a loop of hide or cord tied to its top. An animal steps into the loop and the hunter cuts the sapling loose, which flies up, taking the poor animal with it.

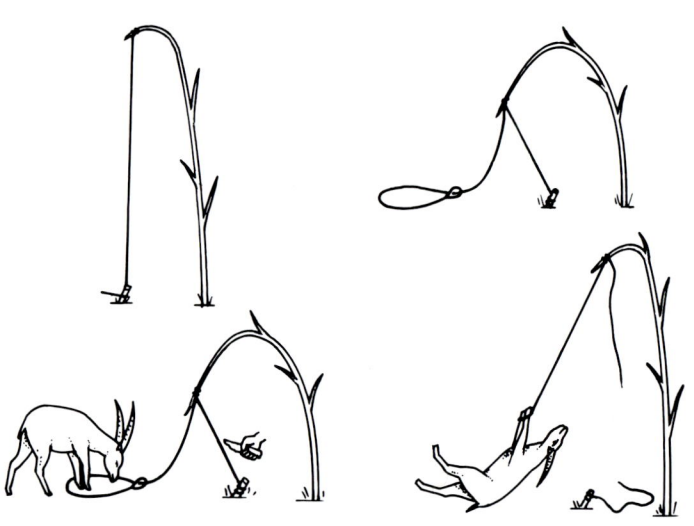

10

▲ A group of Stone Age people gather around a lake. Fresh water is available here and there are fish and birds to catch for food.

make sparks. Or they twisted a stick round and round in a log, by fixing a loop of bow string round the stick and sawing it back and forth to make fire. With fire, people invented ways of melting iron to make better tools and weapons.

Barter and Coins

People long ago did not need to buy anything. They would just exchange things that they had for things that they wanted. Someone who had meat and wanted eggs had to find someone else who had eggs and wanted meat. This was called bartering. It was a very clumsy way of doing things. So **token** goods, which could be exchanged for anything, were invented. Token goods were the earliest form of money. Things that were hard to come by were used, such as salt, iron nails, pots and beads. Some people used cattle as money. Later gold, silver and jewels were used as money. 2,500 years ago King Alyattes of Lydia (part of present-day Turkey) invented the earliest known coin, the stater. The Chinese made the first paper money in the ninth century AD.

Token goods were the first form of money. Necklaces of beads, teeth on rings of metal, and cowrie shells were exchanged. Some peoples in the Pacific still use cowrie shells as money. ▼

THE EARLIEST INVENTIONS

From Yoke to Wheel

Did You Know?
The Egyptians did not need wheeled carts to move heavy loads for they could use boats on the Nile. They used the **lever** and the **inclined plane** or ramp to build their pyramids and temples.

Oxen hitched to a wooden plough could pull a simple digging stick, guided by a ploughman. A single pole linked the plough to a double-yoke so two oxen could pull it. ▼

The North American Indians ▶ used the travois to haul loads with a horse on which they rode.

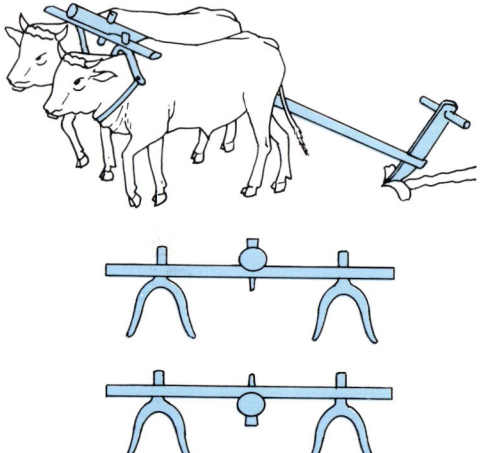

Two big ideas improved the way people moved about on land: the use of animals to move heavy loads, and the wheel. People first tamed cattle around 6000 BC and trained oxen to pull a plough by means of a **yoke** and **harness**. Pack saddles were used to move goods from place to place. The pack saddle may have come from the travois, a pack tied to two poles attached to the animal, with the poles trailing on the ground. It is still used by some Siberian and North American Indian tribes. The sled was also used over smooth ground and on ice or snow. Sleds and rollers were probably used to move heavy objects that could not be broken down into smaller loads.

Roll on the Wheel
The wheeled cart may have first appeared in the cities of **Mesopotamia** (present-day Iraq) around 3500 BC. The carts had **axles** that turned with the wheels, held in place by leather straps. They were smeared with animal grease to help them turn. Similar carts can be found in India to this day. About this time the door was invented. In Sumer someone put the idea of the door **hinge** and the axle together and invented the wheel-and-axle, the first great mechanical invention. Now the axle stayed still and the wheel moved round it.

Water Wheels

Treadmills, driven by men or beasts, were known in Babylonian times. Then someone invented the water wheel to drive the treadmill and it became a water-mill. The idea came from the potter's wheel. Water wheels were used for **irrigating** the land in Ancient **Babylon**. Later the water wheel was linked by toothed wheels to millstones to grind corn and to spindles to lift heavy loads. The Romans used water-driven sawmills to cut logs.

In this Mesopotamian city we ▲ can see oxen pulling an early kind of ox-cart with an axle that turned with the wooden wheels. The movable wheel and fixed axle had not been invented.

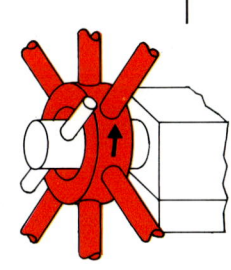

Rotating axle   Fixed axle

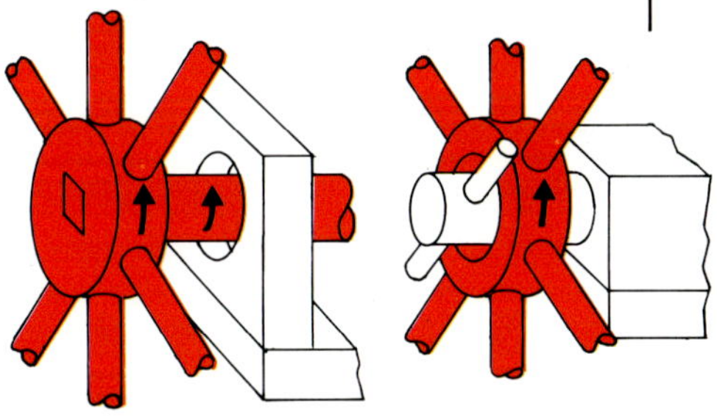

This drawing shows the ▲ difference between a rotating axle and a fixed axle.

◀ This early water-wheel used animal-power to lift water by a series of pegged wheels.

13

THE EARLIEST INVENTIONS

Words and Numbers

Writing and the Alphabet

The **Sumerians** were the first people to develop a form of writing. They used picture **symbols** to stand for things, like cows or arrows. Other words could be shown by using picture symbols of things that sounded the same as the word. We still use the idea in simple rebus puzzles where, for instance, a picture of an eye can stand for the word I. Other picture word systems were used by the Egyptians and the Chinese. The next step was the invention of the alphabet. The **Semites** of Syria and Palestine, and later the **Phoenicians**, invented about thirty signs, each standing for a consonant. The Greeks evolved vowel signs as well. By then any word could be written down easily.

The Invention of Number

People have been counting things since prehistoric times. About the same time as writing was being developed, number systems were invented. The Babylonians, Sumerians, **Mayans**, Chinese and Indians all had number systems. The Chinese invented the abacus, a simple counting device with sliding beads on rods. It is still used today. The greatest number invention, zero, was invented by the Indians in about AD 600. It allowed people to write very large numbers using only the ten symbols 1 to 9 and zero.

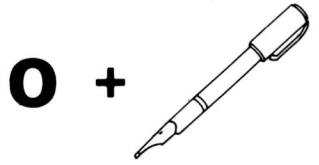

O + pen = open

P + ark = park

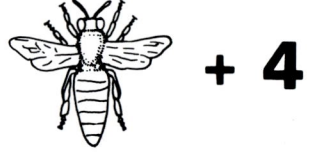

bee + 4 = before

A simple rebus puzzle, ▲ showing how words can be made using picture symbols.

The development of the alphabet is shown here. ▶

Phoenician	Classical Greek	Etruscan	Classical Latin	Modern capitals
⩺	A	⩤	A	A
⬎	B	B	B	B
⇂	Γ	<	C	C
⇃	E	⅋	E	E
⪦	M	M	M	M
W	Σ	⧼	S	S

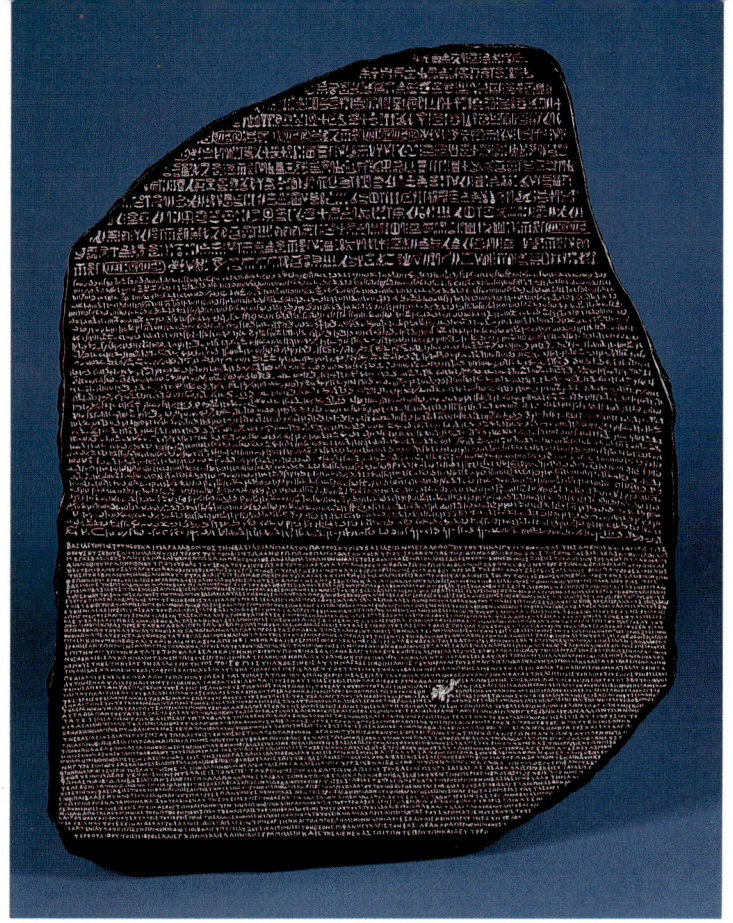

◀ The Rosetta Stone was discovered in 1799 at a small village called Rashîd, or Rosetta, in Egypt. The inscriptions are written in two languages, Egyptian and Greek, but in three scripts: Egyptian hieroglyphs (*top*) and demotic (*middle*), and Greek (*bottom*). As they all read the same, and the Greek language was already known, it was possible to decipher the hieroglyphs for the first time.

Paper-making

Paper gets its name from papyrus, a reed that grows along the Nile. The Egyptians used it for writing on. Paper, as we know it, was invented in China in AD 105 by Ts'ai Lun. He made paper by beating bark from mulberry trees. He also used old fishing nets!

Paper Facts

- Europeans made paper from linen rags for 500 years.

- In 1798, a Frenchman, Nicolas Louis Robert, invented a machine for making paper in long strips, rather than short sheets.

- In 1840 a German, Friedrich Gottlieb Keller, invented a machine for making paper by grinding up logs into a pulp, much as is used in paper-mills today.

◀ A modern Chinese abacus, similar to those used in Ancient China. The beads in the upper part, known as 'Heaven', count as five units each. The lower, larger part was called 'Earth', each bead counting as one. The number stored on this abacus is 1,532,786. To use the abacus you flick the beads you wish to calculate with towards the bar in the middle; the beads at the top and bottom of the frame represent numbers not being used in this calculation. Skilled operators can calculate on an abacus faster than others can on a pocket calculator!

THE EARLIEST INVENTIONS

Cities of the Ancient World

Egyptian Facts

- The Egyptians invented stringed musical instruments such as the harp and **lyre**.
- The Egyptian 'rope-stretchers', as they were called, used knotted rope with 3 knots, 4 knots and 5 knots along the three sides to make a right-angled triangle, helpful in building pyramids.
- The Egyptians invented the *shaduf*, a kind of lever machine, to water the land along the Nile. It is still used today.

The Archimedes Screw was invented by Archimedes about 250 BC. The handle at the top end is turned and water flows up the screw and gushes out at the top end. The screw fits snugly inside a tube. The lower end of the screw is dipped in the water to be raised. It was used in the Nile valley to drain and irrigate the land. ▶

Like the Egyptians and **Cretans** before them, the Greeks built great cities, such as Athens. The Romans founded Rome and Pompeii. The Egyptians invented the **arch**, which came to be used by the Greeks and Romans. They also invented glass blowing. The Greeks used swelling columns of marble to build such temples as the Acropolis. The Romans knew how to build vaulting roofs on their buildings. They also invented the aqueduct, a stone canal for carrying water. They were the first people to build arch bridges.

The Greeks developed the pole **lathe**, driven by foot in a to-and-fro motion. They invented the ruler and compass for accurate drawing. The Egyptians used right-angled triangles to build their pyramids. The Greeks used ideas like this to develop the mathematics of **geometry**.

Great Greek Inventors

The greatest Greek inventor was Archimedes. He invented a device to raise water from a river or pool. It is still used along the banks of the Nile to water the land. Archimedes worked out the laws of the **lever** and **pulleys**. He is said to have constructed many ingenious devices that kept back the Roman invaders for three years at the siege of Syracuse.

Hero of Alexandria invented the **force pump** and the suction pump and a steam-driven

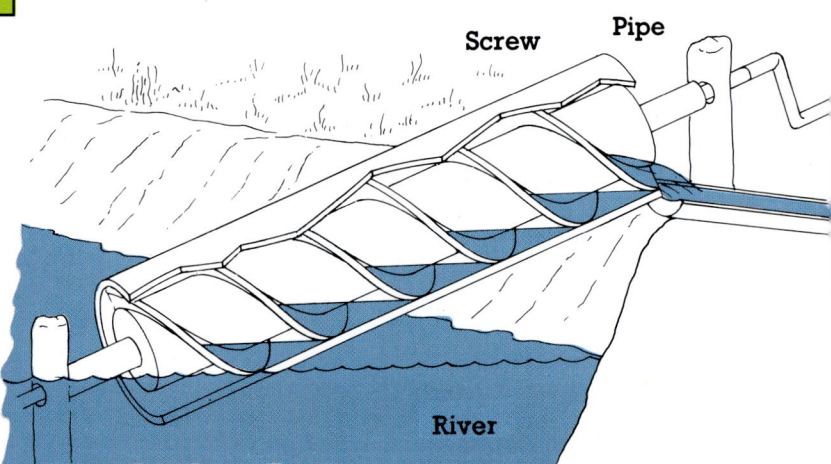

16

toy. The Greeks invented a better kind of *clepsydra*, or water clock, first used in Egypt around 1500 BC, and the hydrometer, which measures the density of liquids.

Roman Inventions

The Romans invented the crane. They were the first to use arches instead of beams in their buildings. They put them up using **block and tackle** and pulleys. They made the first beehives. They used the honey to sweeten their drinks. They invented the surgeon's curette, a special knife used in operations.

▲ This Roman aqueduct was built in the first century AD, at Pont du Gard, France. It is 270 m long and 49 m high.

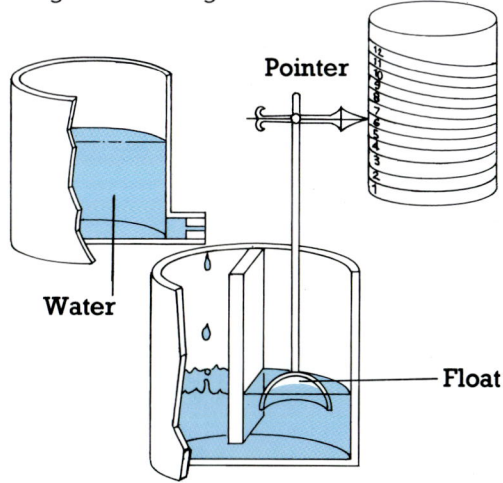

▲ A *clepsydra*, or water-clock, invented by the Greeks. A Chinese water-clock, made in 1088, stood nearly 40 feet high! It showed the passage of the stars as well as the time of day.

◄ A simple *shaduf* on the banks of the Nile. It consists of a long pole, made from a tree, on the end of which hangs a bucket. A bag acts as a counterweight to make lifting easier.

3: INVENTION ON THE MOVE

Early Transport

Getting About on Land

Thanks to the saddle and **stirrup**, invented in India, people could get about more easily and farther afield than ever before. With the horse-collar, invented in China in the sixth century AD, they could move bulk loads farther too. The horse-collar pulled on the animal's shoulders, not across its breast, which would have throttled it. The horse replaced the ox for drawing a plough and the horse-cart replaced the ox-cart. With the invention of nailed horse-shoes, used in Rome around 100 BC, horses could pull wagons along the long straight Roman roads made of stone and cobble. Goods, such as corn, fish, hides, wool, cloth and silk from China, could be hauled to and from country fairs.

From Dug-out to Small Ship

People first built towns along the banks of rivers such as the Nile in Egypt and the Tigris and Euphrates rivers in Mesopotamia. They learned to cross rivers, lakes and even the open sea using logs and blown-up pig bladders as floats. The first boats were **dug-**

A modern blacksmith is seen here shoeing the hind leg of a horse. The nails are hammered in round the hard rim of the horse's hoof. This does not harm the horse in any way. ▼

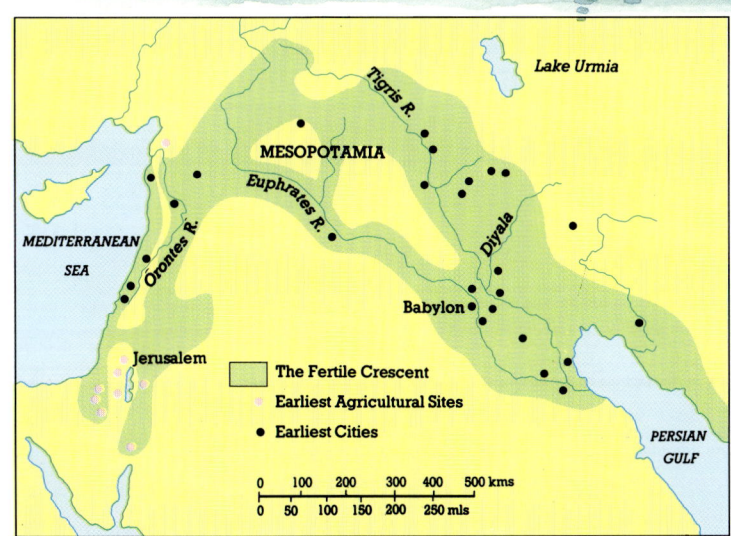

The invention of the sail ▲ greatly increased the range of shipping on the Nile.

◀ A map of Mesopotamia, which means 'between the rivers', that is, the rivers Tigris and Euphrates. The Sumerians lived here between 4000 and 3000 BC.

out canoes and rafts made of reeds and bamboos.

River Boats

The first river boats were flimsy affairs. The Egyptians made boats of reeds for travelling up and down the Nile. They tied a rope from the bow (front) to the stern (back) to keep the ends of the boat from drooping in the water. People could catch fish from their boats and so the fishing net, basket, hook, line and rod came to be invented.

How the Sail was Invented

A man stood up in his boat and opened his arms inside his cloak. A breeze blew him and his boat along the river. The sail was the first mechanical means of taming natural power for man's needs.

INVENTION ON THE MOVE

Sailing Ships

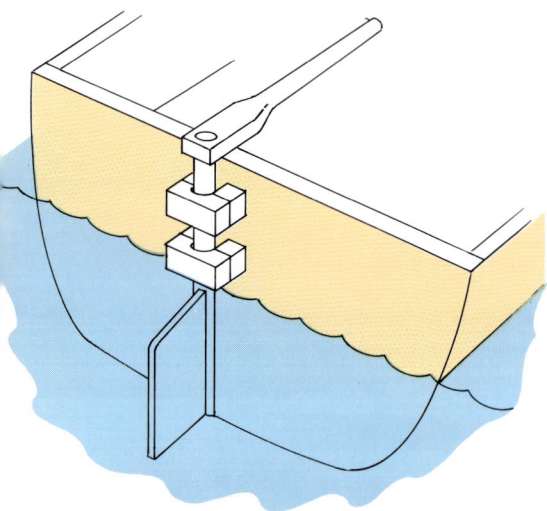

▲ When the tiller, or handle of a rudder is pushed to the left, the rudder moves to the right. The movement of the water past the boat pushes the rudder to the left and the nose of the boat veers right.

Dhows were first sailed off the ▶ coast of East Africa by the Arabs in about AD 1000 and still are.

The first sailors were probably the Cretans. They sailed over the Mediterranean Sea in open galleys driven by oars around 3000 BC. Also around this time the Polynesians may have been travelling from island to island across the Pacific Ocean. The Egyptians were exploring the Nile in their river boats. By 1500 BC the Phoenicians had invented the use of planks to make sea-going ships called biremes. They had two banks of oars each side and a sail. From these came the Greek and Roman galleys. The Greeks invented the long ship, driven by sails and oars. They were excellent sailors and brought back new inventions from their travels abroad. They discovered **magnetite** in Magnesia, a part of Asia Minor, from which comes the word magnet. The Greek Anachasis invented the ship's two-headed anchor in about 800 BC.

Long boat and Rudder

By about AD 800 the Vikings had invented their long boats with a **keel** and sloping back and sides. Steering was done by an oar fixed to the starboard, or 'steer board' side. Around AD 1100 the Chinese invented the **stern-post** rudder, which they fixed to the rear of their flat-bottomed junks. When it was discovered how to fit a rudder to the long ship's sloping back sailors could sail farther than ever before. By AD 1300 merchants from Genoa in Italy were sailing back and forth to the North Sea.

▲ This Greek vase is around 2500 years old. It shows a merchant ship, which only has sails, and a warship, which also has oars.

◀ A Viking longboat. Vikings sailed across the Atlantic as far as Greenland.

This early map of the world was made in about AD 40. ▼

Map-making

Using a sail, ships could easily travel out of sight of land. As a result the sailors had to find their way by the stars. At this time the sea chart was invented. Men also made maps of the land and of the stars in the sky. By sighting the stars and using a land map sailors could make landfall wherever they wanted to. So began the science of **navigation**.

INVENTION ON THE MOVE

Finding the Way

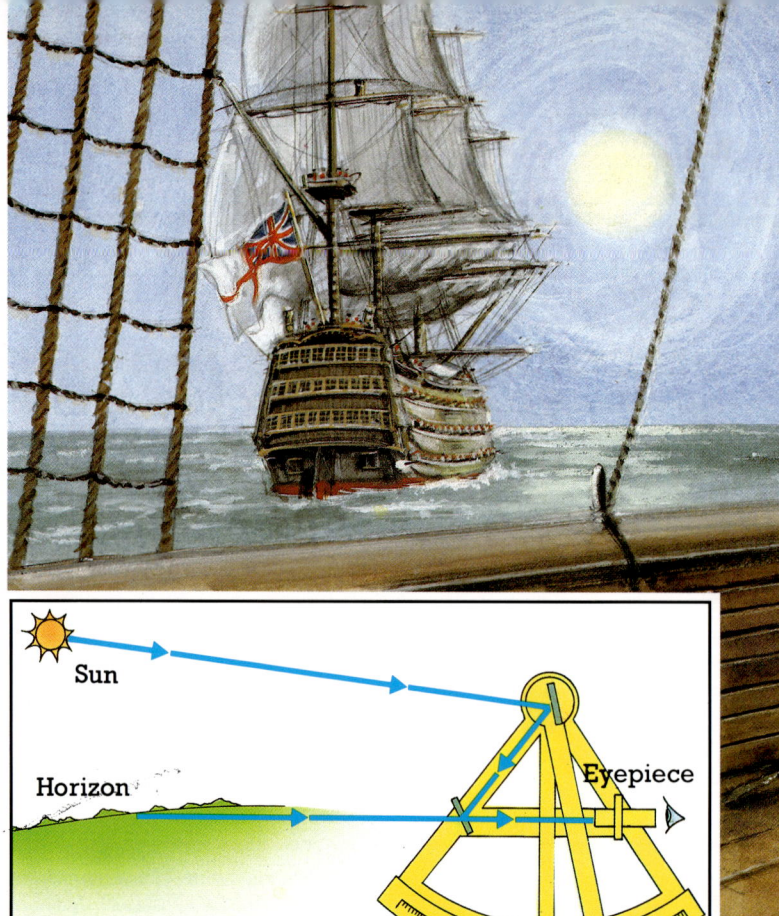

This astrolabe was made in 1548 by George Hartman of Nuremberg, in Germany.

The Chinese found that a chunk of lodestone, a magnetic form of iron, when pivoted on a needle always points north. Around AD 1200 European sailors used lodestones as ship's compasses to find their way around the Mediterranean Sea. The pieces of lodestone were supported on cork, which floated in a dish of water. The **compass card** was first invented in the thirteenth century AD. The invention of the ship's compass improved navigation, making long sea voyages possible. This threw the oceans open for exploration. Before the invention of the compass sailors navigated by means of the astrolabe. This may have been invented by the Greek Hipparchus around 150 BC. It was used on board ship by medieval navigators even after the invention of the compass. It was pointed at the stars to measure their angles above the horizon. From this the navigator could work out the position of the ship. The astrolabe was also used for surveying the land. Sailors also used a crude

| Lodestone |
| Needle |

> ## Using a Sextant
> With a sextant the ship's navigator 'shoots the sun' through the smoked glass of a telescope. He lines up by means of mirrors a point on the horizon. The angle to the sun is shown on a graded scale like that on a school protractor.

◀ The lodestone of a compass pivots on a needle. The navigator can read the direction from the compass card. ▼

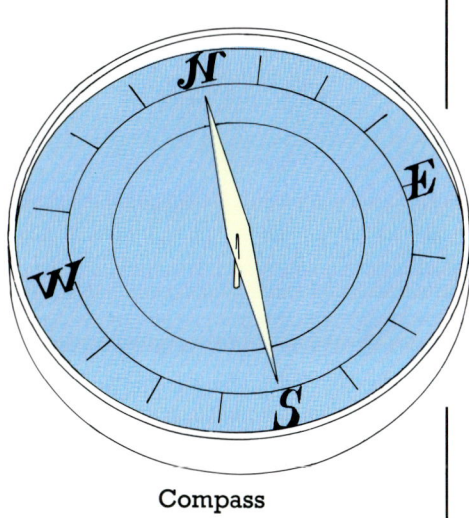

Compass

kind of sextant called a **cross staff**. The telescope improved sea navigation enormously. It gave sailors more accurate sightings of landmarks or the stars. To pin-point a ship's position at sea sailors needed to know the precise time. They used the **nocturnal**, a kind of **protractor** for shooting the stars. Really accurate time-keeping wasn't possible until the invention of the chronometer (see page 33).

The Sextant
The sextant was invented by John Hadley in England and Thomas Godfrey in the United States. It is used to measure the angle between the sun or a star and a point on the horizon. Navigators use it to find the position of their ship. Accurate navigation meant that cargoes could be sent round the world with confidence of their arriving at their intended port.

4: INVENTIONS FOR WAR

Slings and Catapults

All through history people have invented bigger and better weapons and machines of war. One of the simplest inventions for killing was the sling. A sling is really a lever, an extension of a person's arm, to give the shot greater speed. About 3000 BC in Sumer, crude four-wheeled chariots were used to carry spear-throwers into battle. In 1100 BC the Persians invented the two-wheeled war chariot. It had an axle and very accurately made **spokes** so horses could pull it rapidly.

Swords and Armour

Soon after someone invented bronze (an **alloy** of copper and tin) the sword was also invented. Greek and Roman soldiers wore heavy suits of armour. The Romans developed the early **battering ram**. They used a huge tree trunk tipped with metal and swung on ropes like a **pendulum**. They also used scaling ladders for climbing city walls. The Roman engineer Vitruvius designed a fighting tower over thirty metres high, armoured with boards and animal hides. It had many levels and a massive battering ram at its base.

This Roman soldier is ▲ equipped for battle. He has body-armour of iron bands fastened to a leather lining. He also has a bronze helmet and a large shield.

Fighting Facts

The fighting tower was invented by the Assyrians around 900 BC.

● The cross-bow, a development of the bow and arrow, was invented by the Chinese around 500 BC.

24

Catapults

The Greeks used catapults in the fourth century BC. Alexander the Great used a catapult at the siege of Tyre in 332 BC. It could fire stones or arrows. In the tenth century AD the Chinese invented the trebuchet, a giant sling-shot machine for hurling missiles. It worked by means of **counterweights**. It was used in Europe by the early twelfth century. The onager, a smaller kind of catapult, was invented by the Romans. A lever was pulled back against the pull of twisted ropes. When let go, it could hurl a rock hundreds of metres.

▲ This stone carving shows an Assyrian chariot of around 870 BC. It had an axle that turned freely inside the wheel hub. It was built by skilled wheelwrights who fashioned the many spokes that support the wheel rim from the hub. The chariot was driven by a single warrior-driver, and was pulled by four horses who could go up to nearly 40 mph at full gallop. The chariot was low-slung to prevent its turning over when taking corners too sharply.

◄ This siege catapult is being wound back ready to hurl a rock at the castle walls. Long lever arms help the men to pull the catapult arm back against the pull of tightly twisted ropes. Sinew or hair were also used instead of rope. When pulled back to its full extent, the catapult arm was locked, ready to be released.

INVENTIONS FOR WAR

Gunpowder and Cannons

The Chinese invented gunpowder, the oldest explosive known to man, around the ninth century AD. They used it only for fireworks and rockets. Roger Bacon, a scholar of Oxford University, wrote about gunpowder in 1242 after its arrival in Europe. It was to change people's lives and methods of warfare totally. It was used to fire cannon balls from cannons.

Cannons on Land

Cannons eventually replaced the catapult and the battering ram, not because they had a greater range but because, for all their clumsiness and cost, they were still cheaper and easier to move. In Europe cannons revolutionized warfare on land. Cannon balls could batter down castle walls. Smaller cannons, like the hand-held musket, were also deadly weapons. They gave their users greater fire-power in battles.

Cannons at Sea

At sea the use of gunpowder had no less an impact. Its use replaced the traditional methods of fighting at sea – ramming and boarding and setting fire. Ships in the **Middle Ages** carried cannons for blasting enemy craft out of the water; they were also used to transport cannons, unfired, from place to place. Ships' cannons enabled European ships to command the high seas and to plunder the resources of other lands. This the Spaniards and the Portuguese did in South America and in Mexico from the sixteenth century AD.

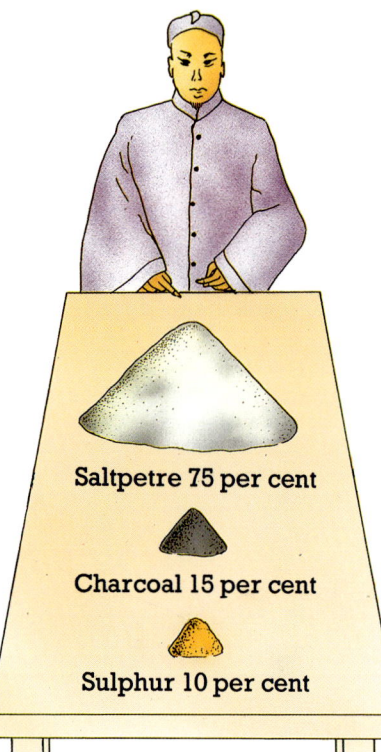

▲ The Chinese made gunpowder from sulphur, charcoal and saltpetre (potassium nitrate). The saltpetre makes the mixture burn well – so well it explodes!

A cutaway drawing of a musket. This was really a small hand-held cannon. ▶

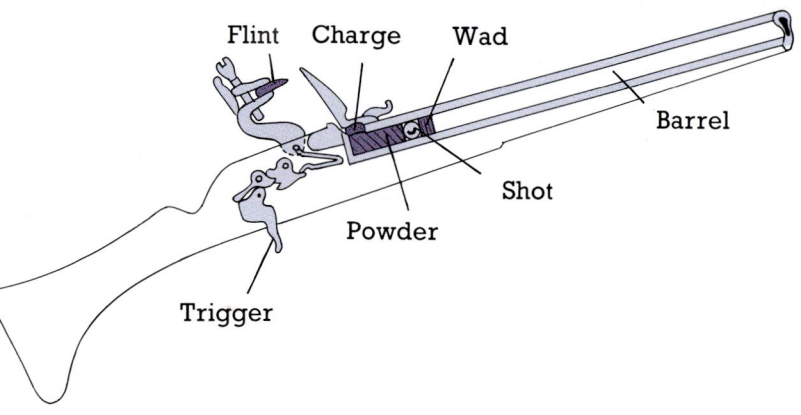

The Big Bang in Science

Gunpowder made an even greater impact on science than on warfare. The making of gunpowder hastened the development of laboratory skills, invented by the **alchemists**, and as a result gave a boost to the development of chemistry, which had grown out of alchemy.

Scientists tried to predict the flight of the cannon ball and to improve the explosive force of the charge. Out of these attempts grew the science of **ballistics** and explosives. The boring of cannon barrels led to advances in the science of heat. From these humble beginnings grew the great inventions of the Industrial Revolution (see Chapter 6).

▲ In battles at sea the captain of the flagship tried to station his ships so the wind was blowing behind him. Most of the guns on board fired out of the sides of the ships.

Gunners needed to know the flight of a cannon ball to be able to aim it successfully at their target. The gunners' rules of thumb for hitting the target led to the more accurate science of ballistics, or gunnery. ▼

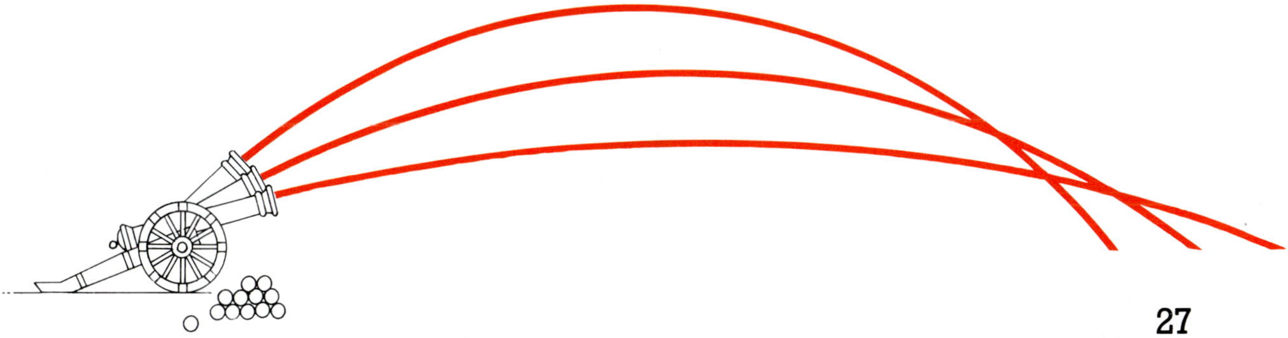

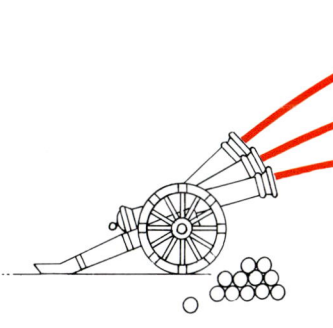

5: THE ADVANCE OF SCIENCE

Leonardo da Vinci

Leonardo da Vinci (1452-1519) was artist, master craftsman, architect and engineer all rolled into one. He was also an inventor – perhaps the greatest genius of the **Renaissance**. He filled many of his notebooks with his inventions. All were way ahead of his time. His notebooks showed how keenly he studied what he'd seen metal-workers and engineers do. He mastered mechanics and hydraulics, the science of water flow. But, alas, not all of his inventions would have worked – even had he been able to find the money to build them. Why? Because he did not know enough mathematics and science to design them properly; nor, come to that, did he have the mechanical power of the steam-engine or petrol engine to drive his inventions.

Leonardo's Inventions

His greatest invention on paper was his flying machine. He made mechanical models after watching the flight of birds. After making many calculations he made some full-scale trials with a model. His plans for his inventions were all superbly drawn. They include:

- An armoured car driven by a man pedalling within it, and turning cranks connected to the wheels.
- A *clotonbrot*, a shell packed with gunpowder and iron balls.
- An alarm clock that woke the sleeper up by tilting the bed he lay on!
- A submarine for going under water.

Backward Writing

Leonardo da Vinci wrote 7,000 pages of notes. He could use both hands equally well. He wrote most of his notes backwards with his left hand. He then read them with a mirror.

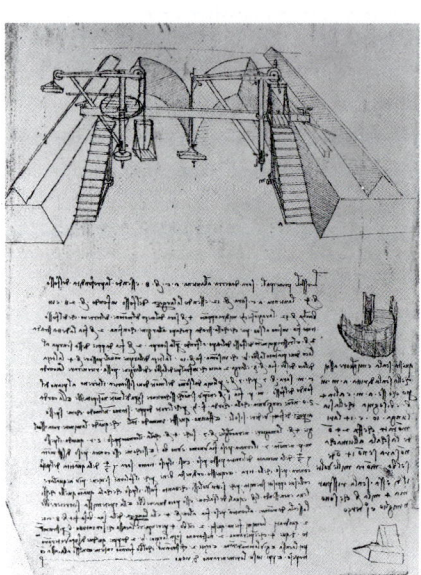

▲ This is a page from one of Leonardo's notebooks. In the notebooks he made sketches of his ideas and inventions.

Leonardo's flying machine, ▲ shown in his notebooks, is here shown created out of wood in 1988. It looks, from above, rather like a bird's wing. Unfortunately, it would never fly.

Leonardo worked for some of the most powerful princes of his day, such as Lorenzo the Magnificent and Cesare Borgia. He died in the service of King Francis I of France.

◀ Leonardo da Vinci was not only a great painter and architect, but a designer and inventor. He also studied geology, biology and mathematics and carried out simple experiments on human vision. He could work a brass foundry, too.

- A diving suit to enable a man to stay under water for four hours.
- A crude sort of helicopter.
- Force pumps for lifting water out of mines.
- Rolling-mills for flattening and shaping metal into sheets.
- A mobile canal-cutter.

THE ADVANCE
OF SCIENCE

From Near and Far

Telescopes and Microscopes
As the invention of the telescope opened up the world of the stars and planets and the very big, so that of the microscope revealed the world of **microbes** and the very small.

From Eye-glass to Spyglass
The Arabs discovered how to grind glass lenses, and how to focus light rays with a magnifying glass. By 1350 people in Italy were wearing eye-glasses, or spectacles. Then one day around 1600 something remarkable happened.

An apprentice in the workshop of Hans Lippershey, a Dutch lens grinder, looked through two lenses in the shop window and saw that they made things outside look nearer. And so was invented the telescope. In the hands of the great scientist Galileo this was to prove the greatest scientific instrument of the age. Galileo built his first telescope around 1610.

▲ Early glasses were simple in shape and of few sizes. The spectacles shown here date from the early 1500s.

The simple type of refracting telescope is called the *Galilean*, after the famous **astronomer**. The big lens gathers light and forms a magnified image of the object being looked at. The reflecting telescope (*below*) has a mirror instead of a lens to gather light from the object. One kind of reflecting telescope is called the *Newtonian* after the famous scientist. ▶

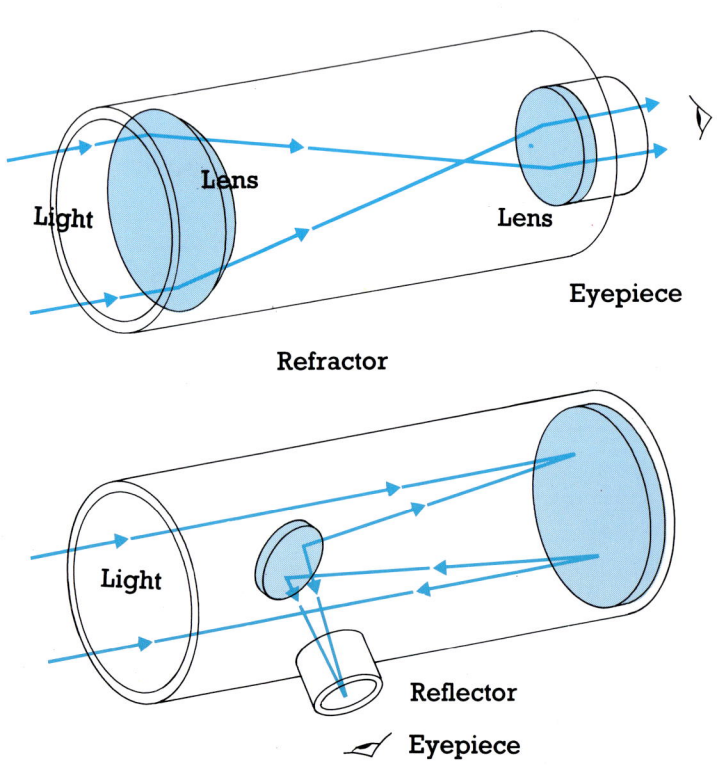

Antony van Leeuwenhoek (1632-1723) used tiny lenses he ground himself to reveal a new world of the very small. He made hundreds of lenses that magnified up to 270 times. With these lenses he studied stagnant water, scrapings from teeth, blood cells, and muscle fibres. To make the microscope shown he put a tiny lens between two sheets of brass. He put specimens he wanted to look at on a thin rod that could be screwed up or down.

The World of Small Things

A Dutch spectacle-maker, Zacharias Janssen, is credited with the invention of the first compound microscope in 1590. A Dutch draper in Delft, Antony van Leeuwenhoek (say it 'Lay-ven-hook'), ground tiny but perfect lenses that magnified over 200 times. His simple microscope showed things that had never been seen before. He saw water fleas and other tiny **organisms** that live in water. He even studied bacteria with it. But the microscope, unlike the telescope, was not seen as having any immediate practical use. It was ignored until 200 years later when the French scientist Louis Pasteur used it to combat disease.

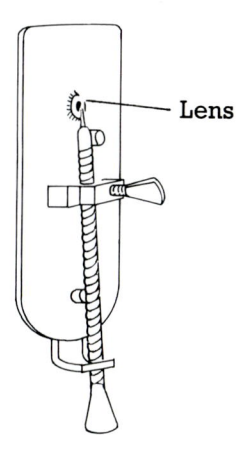
Lens

THE ADVANCE OF SCIENCE

Telling the Time

Galileo is seen here swinging a simple pendulum. With a thread the length shown, about a metre, the period of swing is about 2 seconds. ▼

The very first clocks were sundials, which told the time by shadows cast by the sun. Then came burning candles marked off in hours, water-clocks, and the hour-glass or sand-timer. The first clockwork machines may have been geared astrolabes. In the late Middle Ages the escapement was invented; this enabled the gears to move at a steady rate. A device with an escapement thus became the first clockwork clock. Churches had clocks like these. They rang a bell to tell the watchman to ring the church bell. From this comes our word 'watch'. The earliest known mechanical clock was built in the chapel tower of the Visconti Palace in Milan, in 1335.

Pendulum Clocks

Galileo thought of the idea of a pendulum to keep time for a clock. The great Dutch scientist Christian Huygens invented the pendulum clock. A heavy weight, or bob, on the end of a

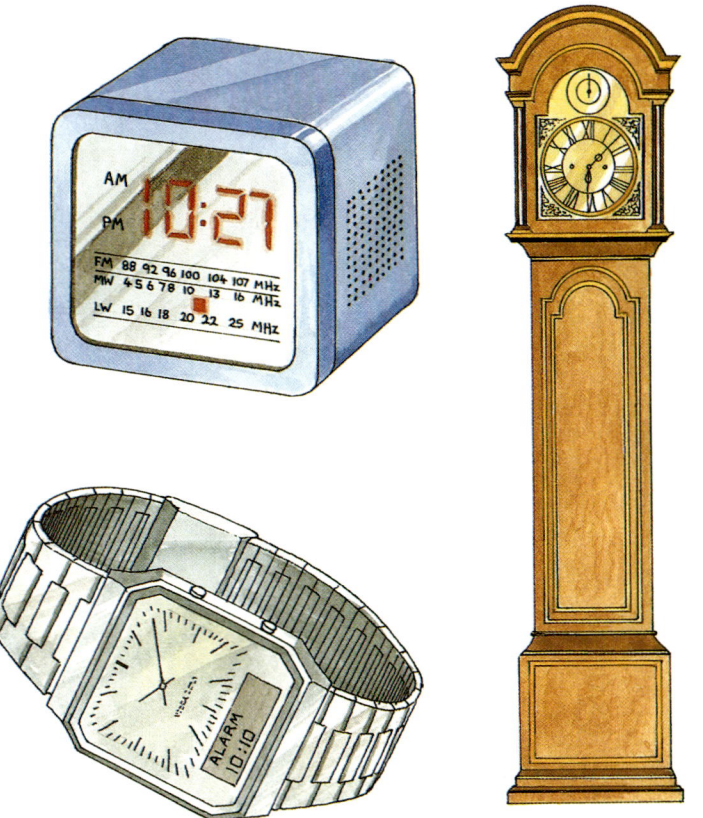

◀ An assortment of clocks that have been invented through the ages: a candle clock, an hourglass, a sundial, a digital radio clock, a wristwatch, and a grandfather clock.

The clock in Salisbury ▲ Cathedral is the oldest clock that still works. It was made of iron in 1386. It ticks once every 4 seconds. The ropes round the drums drive the clock round.

John Harrison solved the problem of finding longitude at sea. He built the first really accurate timepieces that could be used successfully at sea. The chronometer shown was the fourth he designed. ▼

rope is wound round a spindle linked by cogs to the clockwork. An escapement mechanism controls the speed of fall of the bob so that the clock ticks at a steady rate.

Navigation and the Chronometer

Inventions of timepieces went on apace. Why? Because, to pin-point a ship's position at sea accurately, sailors needed to know the precise time. Robert Hooke, an English scientist, replaced the pendulum by precision clockwork, and so he invented the chronometer. But it was a long time before a chronometer that would keep perfect time at sea was invented. This was achieved by a carpenter, John Harrison, in 1764. Harrison's chronometer was not much larger than a pocket watch, yet it kept time to within one-tenth of a second per day! With his chronometer sailors could accurately tell the time at sea and so work out their exact position.

THE ADVANCE OF SCIENCE

Water-mills and Windmills

A feature of life in the Middle Ages was the water-mill. In almost every manor was a mill and a miller. Some 5,000 of them are listed in the **Domesday Book**. As well as for grinding corn, the water-mill was used for hammering. This use depended on the **trip-hammer** and the crank, both Chinese inventions. It was also used for drawing thin copper wire. The crank was one of the most important mechanical inventions devised.

Windmills

The windmill, invented perhaps, by the Persians, was used in China and elsewhere for grinding corn and irrigating the land in the tenth century AD. With it people had invented another way of harnessing wind-power.

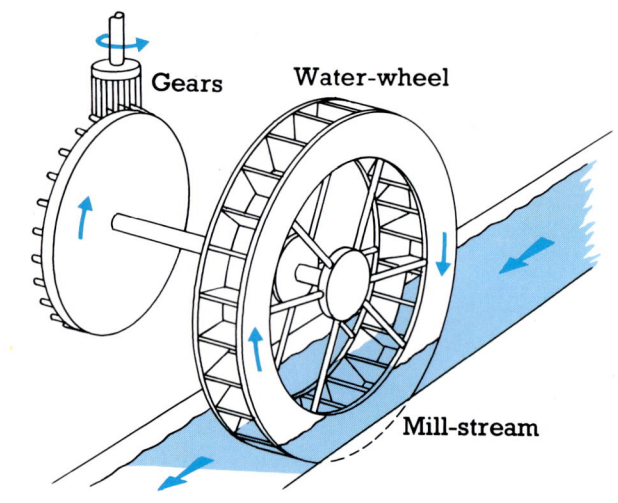

The undershot water-wheel shown here is turned by the fast-running water striking the blades of the wheel at the bottom. It has such a low efficiency that overshot wheels are preferred. ▶

The typical medieval manor house had a water-wheel. It was used to turn machinery inside the house, such as roasting spits. The water from a stream would be diverted into a bricked channel to increase the water's speed and depth. ▶

◀ Windmills like this one at Kinderdyk in Holland were once used to pump water or turn millstones to grind corn. The four sails of the windmill are made of wooden slats that catch the wind and turn the sails round.

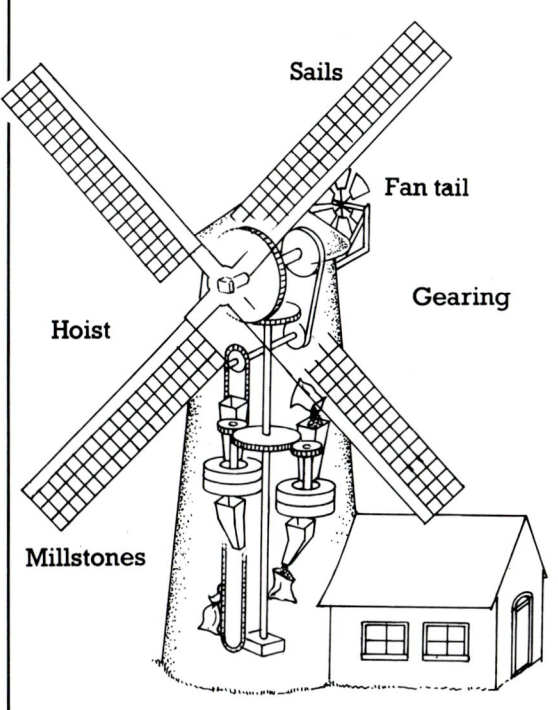

Windmills found their way to Europe by 1150. They were used for fulling (beating and washing) cloth, for blowing bellows into furnaces, for forging iron, and for sawing wood. And, of course, for grinding corn.

By the twelfth century AD windmills and water-mills were in wide use throughout the flatlands of Europe, such as Northern France, Holland, Belgium and Spain. Later, in the Industrial Revolution, windmills were used in England for spinning and weaving cloth and for threshing corn.

Millwrights were men who went round the country making and mending mills. They were craftsmen inventors. They had a hand in making the first clockwork clocks and later in developing machinery in the Industrial Revolution. Wind power was an important source of energy until the invention of the steam-engine.

▲ The sketch of the windmill shown here shows how the sails turn. The top of the windmill is turned into the wind by the fan shown at the back. It works much like a weather cock. When the sails are lined up facing the wind, the wind hits the four sails, spinning them round in a clockwise direction. A series of cogs and gears transfers this power to the millstones.

THE ADVANCE OF SCIENCE

From Printing to Air Pressure

Early Printing
The Chinese invented printing by wood block about AD 770. In AD 1040 Pi Sheng, a Chinese printer, made movable type from clay. The Chinese printed large numbers of Buddhist prayers cheaply. Printing took off in Europe when cheap copies were needed of playing cards.

Otto von Guericke made a test that was one of the most exciting that scientists have ever made. He decided to show the world how strong a vacuum is. He had two teams of horses in the German Emperor's park try to pull the two half globes apart, the only thing holding them together being air pressure. The horses couldn't do it! ▶

Printing
Around 1440 Johannes Gutenberg, a goldsmith of Mainz, in Germany, invented printing using movable type – a process whereby letters of the alphabet are cast from metal and are then put together in a frame (a galley) to make words. Gutenberg could print different pages of a book using the same pieces of type over and over again. He also invented the printing press, probably getting the idea from the wine press. Gutenberg's Bible is one of the most beautiful books ever printed. He used colour in a few copies of the Bible, which he first printed in the 1450s.

Galileo
Galileo invented the pulsometer, a portable pendulum to time the pulse rate of medical patients. He also invented the water thermometer using a glass bulb the size of a hen's egg with a long stem the thickness of a straw. In 1724 Gabriel Daniel Fahrenheit invented the mercury thermometer. Galileo's pupil Evangelista Torricelli invented the **barometer**. He used a glass tube filled with mercury.

Other Inventions
In 1642 Blaise Pascal, a French mathematician and **philosopher**, invented the adding machine. It worked using a system of interlocking cog wheels like the milometer on a bicycle.

◀ Johannes Gutenburg was the inventor of printing in Europe. The picture shows Gutenburg displaying a sheet he has just printed on his press to two friends. He used such a press to print the Bible.

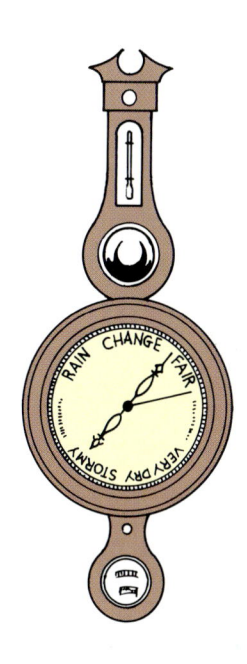

Otto von Guericke devised an air pump to make a **vacuum**. In 1654 he carried out a famous experiment. He pumped all the air out of two half-globes of copper. Having no air pressure left inside, they were held together by the outside air pressure. Two teams of eight dray horses failed to pull the **hemispheres** apart. They are known as the Magdeburg hemispheres after the town in Germany where von Guericke designed the hemispheres. Von Guericke also worked out how to transfer power through long tubes from which air had been pumped and devised a machine for making static electricity using **friction**.

▲ Barometers like this one are often used in people's homes to predict the weather from changes in the pressure of the atmosphere.

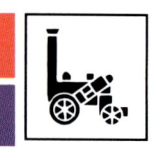

6: THE INDUSTRIAL REVOLUTION

Coal-mining and the Age of the Engine

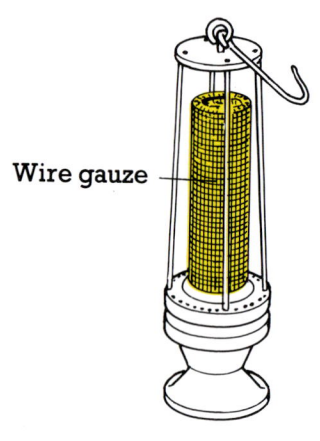

The Industrial Revolution saw the rise of factories in the mid 1700s, first in Britain, then in Germany, then in North America. Country people moved in masses to overcrowded towns. It was the great age of invention. For manufacturers were ready to back inventions with cash!

The increasing use of machinery called for ever more wood to make the machines. But wood quickly wore out. Iron lasted longer, but had to be smelted. To smelt iron huge fires were needed. To feed the fires wood was needed. But many of the forests in Europe and North America had been cut down. So instead coal was used, which had to be dug out of the ground and transported to the smelting ovens. And the mines had to be kept dry from the water that often leaked in. These two problems had to be solved at once. Horses were used to haul coal-wagons. But how to keep the coal-mines dry? New machinery was urgently needed. Several inventors tried to crack the problem.

▲ The miner's safety lamp invented by Sir Humphrey Davy. The metal gauze prevents the heat of the flame from igniting explosive gases.

This is what it used to be like down a mine. The coal had to be hewn out of the coal-face by muscle power. Now it is all done by machines. ▶

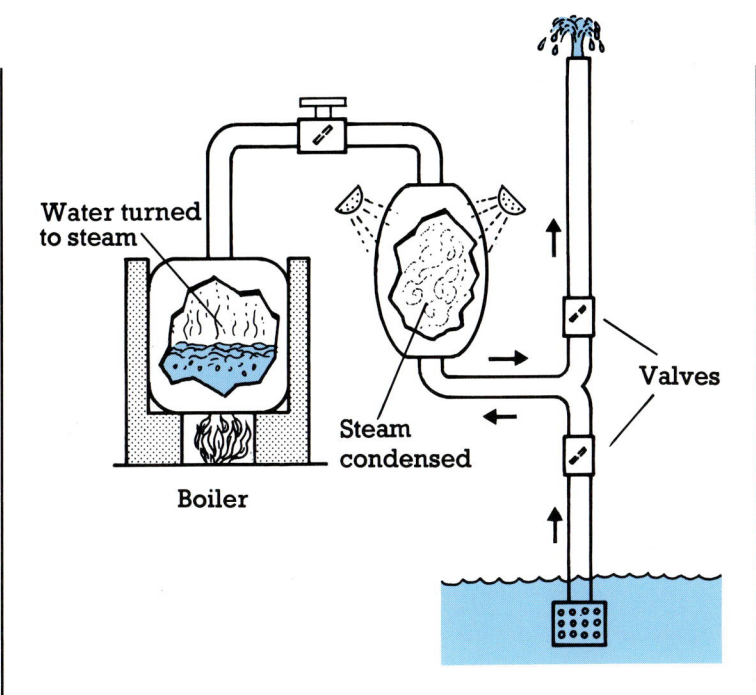

◀ The diagram shows Savery's steam-engine at work, pumping out water from a mine shaft. The pump used two vessels alternately filled with steam to drive water out and then cooled to draw up more water.

'The Miner's Friend'

In 1698 Captain Thomas Savery of London patented a steam-driven pumping engine. He knew well the importance of his invention, saying 'that in a few years it will double, if not treble the wealth of this kingdom'. He called it 'The Miner's Friend' because it was designed to pump water from the mines where they worked, making their lives safer and less uncomfortable.

Rocking Beam Engine

In 1712 Thomas Newcomen, an ironmonger of Dartmouth, England, designed a better engine. It had a massive wooden cross-beam. His rocking beam steam-engine was sited at the top of the mine shaft. It was used first for pumping water out of Cornish tin-mines. But it used vast amounts of coal. James Watt was to design a much more efficient steam-engine.

The Davy Lamp

Humphrey Davy, scientist, snob and showman, invented the miner's safety lamp in 1815. The lamp was safe to use in coal-mines where the risk of **fire damp** explosions was great. A naked flame would explode the 'fire damp' gas that was produced in the mines.

▲ Here is a cutaway view of Thomas Newcomen's rocking beam steam-engine in use in a pumping house above a coal-mine shaft. It is being used to pump water out of the shaft. Unlike Savery's engine, it did not have to be built at the bottom of the mine shaft.

THE INDUSTRIAL REVOLUTION

The Age of Steam

The Steam-engine

One day in 1763, James Watt, an instrument maker of Glasgow, Scotland, was repairing a small model of a Newcomen engine. Why was it so inefficient? The answer came to him in a flash when out on a walk. The steam was both heated *and* cooled in the one cylinder. Why not lead the steam off to cool in *another* cylinder? This he built, calling it the 'condenser'. It worked! Watt patented this invention and the modern steam-engine was born. He also patented the governor, which makes an engine work at a constant speed. Watt's steam-engine was a success as a stationary engine. But it did not work at high enough pressures to drive a moving steam locomotive.

The Steam Locomotive

Richard Trevithick, an Englishman, built a high pressure steam-powered carriage in 1801. It was used in the coalfields. It fell to a colliery fireman's son, George Stephenson, to make the final improvement: he made the exhaust steam go out of a funnel. This fanned the flames of the fire in the fire-box and gave the engine enough power to move a locomotive along a track. The age of the railway had arrived with the steam locomotive.

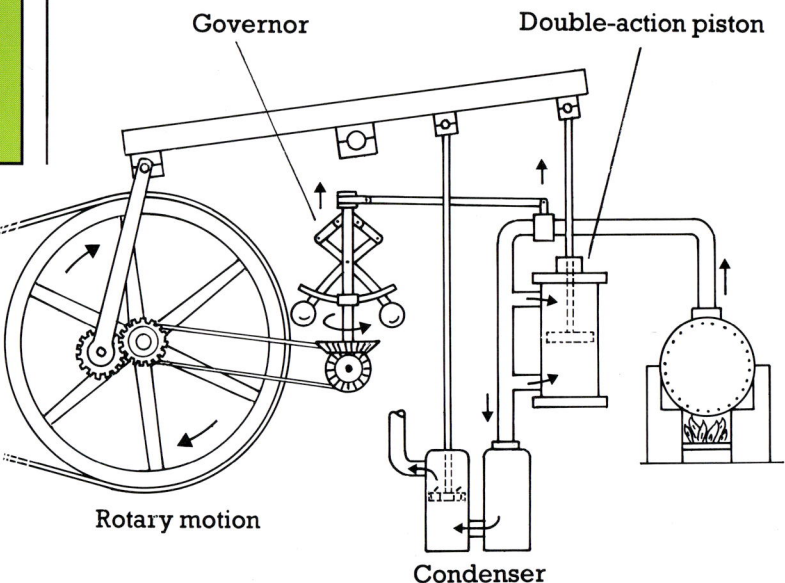

Travel Facts

- John Loudon McAdam introduced a new road surface, **tar macadam**, in 1815. It had a top surface of tar or asphalt. Macadamized roads helped speed up trade.

- Richard Trevithick's steam-engine ran on metal rails. It could carry a load of 20 tons. But it moved very slowly.

- George Stephenson's most famous locomotive, or 'Puffing Billy', was his black-and-yellow Rocket. It reached the dizzying speed of 20 mph!

James Watt's steam-engine used a separate condenser to cool the steam after use in the main cylinder. This enabled the main cylinder to remain hot and so increasing its efficiency. The secret was the double-action piston. ▶

GEO. STEPHENSON'S ROCKET, 1829.

Steamboats

In 1707, Denis Papin invented a steam-powered paddle-wheel boat. When he tried to sail it angry boatmen wrecked it because they feared it would take work from them.

In 1807 Robert Fulton, an American jeweller and portrait-painter, built the first steam-powered boat, or steamer, to carry paying passengers. It was called the *Clermont*. He copied the idea from another American inventor, John Fitch, who built the first steamer on the Delaware River in 1787.

▲ The picture shows a typical early locomotive engine, or 'Puffing Billy'.

Sea-going Facts

- John Fitch invented the steamer passenger boat. But no one was interested in his idea. He died penniless.

- The *Clermont* was the first paying passenger steamer.

- The screw propeller was invented by Richard Trevithick and John Ericsson.

- The first steamer to cross the Atlantic was the *Savannah*. It was fitted with two paddle wheels. It crossed the Atlantic in 1819 in a record-breaking 29 days!

◀ The *Clermont*, first passenger carrying steamship.

THE INDUSTRIAL REVOLUTION

The Spinning Industry

A Cottage Industry

The Industrial Revolution made the biggest impact on the textile (cloth) industry. In the 1700s, land-owners in the West Indies and later North America began growing the cotton shrub. Slaves picked the cotton. It was shipped to Lancashire, England. There, in humble cottages, workers wove the cotton fibre into cloth. So began the weaving industry, as a 'cottage industry'.

The Textile Revolution

Very soon steam power revolutionized this cottage industry into the mighty textile industry, the mainstay of British wealth. The revolution gathered pace at amazing speed as better spinning machines were invented, such as the 'spinning jenny', Richard Arkwright's spinning frame, and the 'spinning mule'.

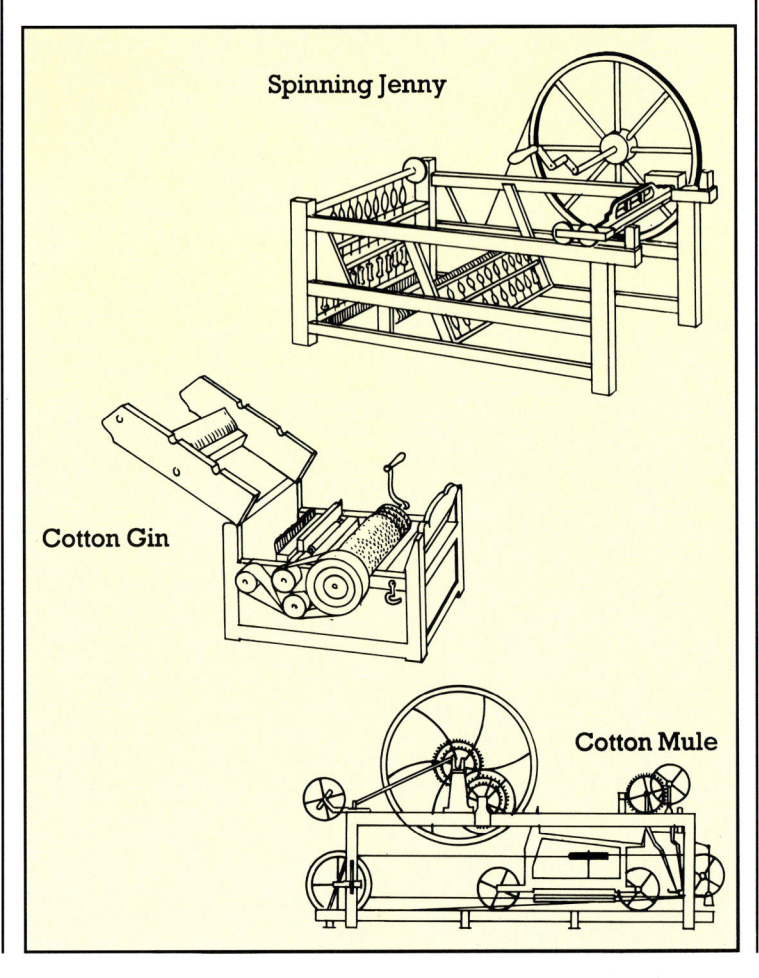

The 'spinning jenny' ('jenny' was a nickname for 'gin' or 'engine') was invented about 1767 by James Hargreaves, a Lancashire weaver. A person operating Hargreaves' spinning jenny could spin 16 or more threads at a time. The spindles were mounted vertically and were turned by a hand-wheel. But the spinning jenny only turned out coarse yarn.

The cotton gin separates cotton fibre from seed. The fibre is fed through a row of saws. Teeth on the saws pull the cotton from the seeds. Richard Arkwright patented the spinning frame in 1769. It was water-powered. It spun mechanically by making motions normally carried out by the human hand. It wove an all-cotton cloth.

In 1779 Samuel Crompton invented the 'spinning mule'. It combined the action of the spinning jenny with that of the spinning frame. It had a set of bobbins, as on a spinning wheel, which moved to and fro, as on a spinning frame. It made very fine yarn.

Spinning Jenny

Cotton Gin

Cotton Mule

Textiles Take Off

In 1789 the textile industry really took off when an English clergyman, Edmund Cartwright, invented the power loom. He used a steam-engine to power a weaving machine that could use the thread being produced by the new machines.

In North America, an English textile mill worker, Samuel Slater, built, in 1793, the first cotton mills for weaving cotton cloth. Cotton manufacturing grew rapidly in America. Also in 1793, Eli Whitney invented the cotton gin. This sorted the cotton fibre from the seed mechanically and speeded up production.

Later Inventions

In 1828 the ring-spinning frame was invented in the USA. More recent inventions include machines for spinning artificial fibres, such as nylon, and the bulking process for producing softer, fluffier **yarns** from artificial fibres.

▲ A textile factory in the late nineteenth century was a grim place. The noise of the weaving and spinning machines was deafening. Here workers, mostly women and some children, had to work long hours from Monday to Saturday, often getting to the factory by 7 in the morning and not leaving till 6 in the evening. The workers were paid a pittance.

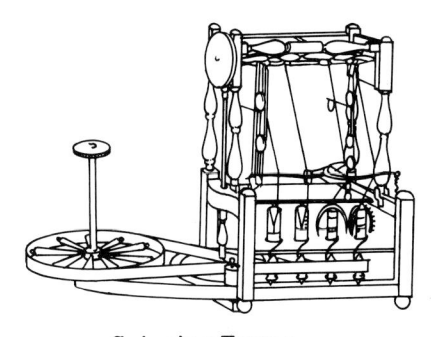

Spinning Frame

THE INDUSTRIAL REVOLUTION

The Metal Revolution

More and better iron and steel were needed to meet the demand for new machinery, including machine tools to make machines. Machines that could cut metals accurately and for making spare parts led to mass production. They all needed high-class steel.

Iron-making

People made iron before they could write. Iron ore was placed in a hot **charcoal** fire. The carbon in the charcoal combined with the oxygen in the iron ore and escaped as carbon dioxide gas. Bellows were used to force air into the fire. Abraham Darby used coke instead of charcoal in blast furnaces to make iron. Air blown by James Watt's steam-engines produced much higher temperatures in the furnace. Henry Cort invented a method of making **wrought-iron** from crude **pig iron**. This was much more pliable and less likely to snap under stress.

The Secret of Steel-making

Cast iron was good enough for making rails, pillars, wheels and bridge girders. But not for making precision tools or the working parts of engines. For these hard, springy steel was needed. Hard steel had been known for four thousand years, but it wasn't until 1722 that a Frenchman, René de Réaumur, solved the mystery of putting carbon in the steel to make it springy. In 1856 Henry Bessemer solved the problem of getting the right amount

Here is a steel-making furnace. Into it are put steel scrap, iron ore and limestone. After these have been heated molten pig iron is added later. When the furnace is charged with the metals great sheets of flame shoot out. Later molten steel is tapped from the furnace. ▶

◄ Iron is made in a blast-furnace. A blast-furnace is a large cylinder made of steel and lined with heat-resistant brick. It is water-cooled to prevent overheating. Molten iron is tapped (drawn off) from the furnace every few hours. Some blast-furnaces can make up to 3,000 tons of iron a day.

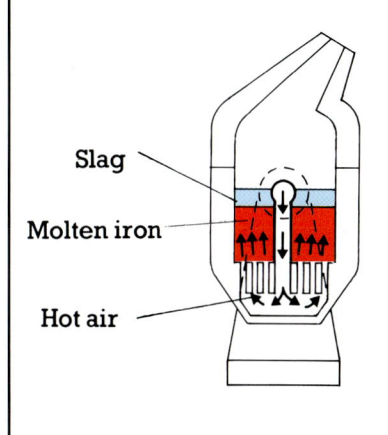

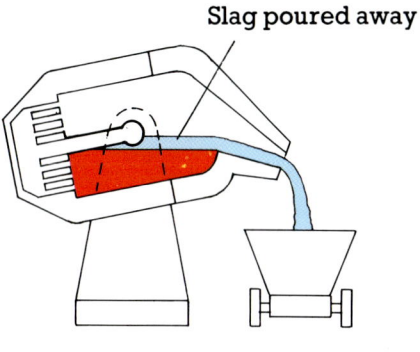

▲ The Bessemer converter is an open-topped furnace shaped a bit like an egg. It may be lined with heat-resistant bricks. The converter is tipped to one side and limestone is added to the molten metal. It is then tipped upright and air is blown into it at high pressure from beneath. This burns out the impurities in the iron.

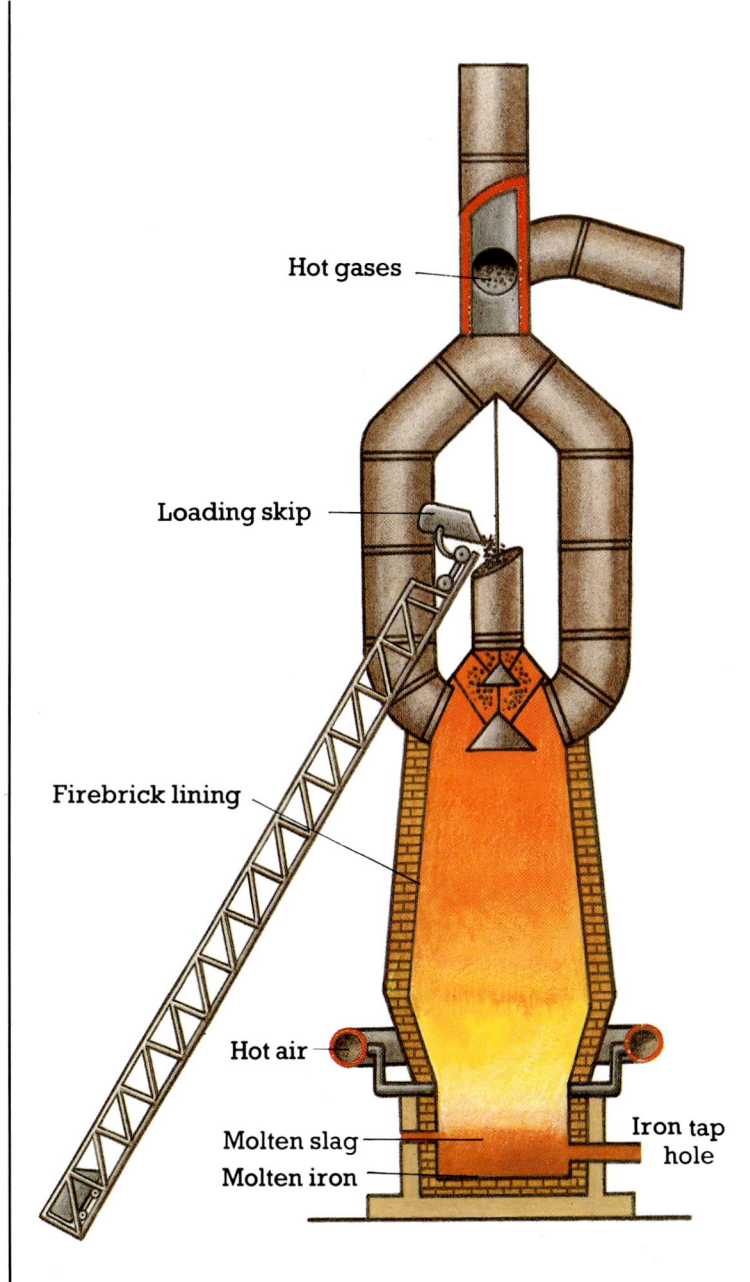

of carbon. He took carbon out of wrought iron with a blast of hot air in his Bessemer converter. In 1878 William Siemens built the first electric arc furnace for steel-making. Both Bessemer's and Siemens' methods could only use pure iron ore. To use impure iron Gilchrist Thomas showed that the furnace must be lined with lime. This removed phosphorus, an impurity, from the iron. After this invention world steel production soared.

THE INDUSTRIAL REVOLUTION

The Age of Electricity

Static Electricity

Comb your hair vigorously and the comb will pick up bits of fluff. This shows static electricity at work. In 1745 a German clergyman, E. J. von Kleist, and later a Dutchman, Pieter von Musschenbroek, made an apparatus for storing static electricity, the Leyden jar. Touching it produced a spark. Benjamin Franklin showed that lightning was the same thing as the Leyden jar's spark, but far more powerful.

Current Electricity

In 1800 an Italian, Alessandro Volta, invented the electric cell (battery). It stored current electricity, not static electricity.

In 1821, Michael Faraday, a great experimenter, once an apprentice to a bookbinder, made current electricity by moving a magnet inside an electric coil. His discovery led to the making of current electricity on a giant scale

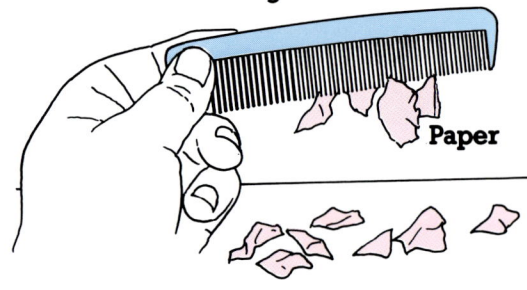

Static electricity can be ▲ made by rubbing a comb through your hair. The comb then becomes charged with negative electricity. When the comb is held near some bits of paper, which have no electric charge, it attracts them and picks them up.

Volta's battery or pile was made up of round discs of copper, zinc and cloth pads soaked in sulphuric acid, arranged in the order copper, acid, zinc, copper, acid, zinc, etc. With many such discs Volta made powerful sparks from the end discs of zinc and copper. ▶

◀ Michael Faraday invented both the electric generator and electric motor. Here he is carrying out an experiment to show how an electric current can be produced from magnetic attraction.

by electric generators. By the 1890s electricity was being used to light up whole cities.

Uses of Electricity

Electricity was used to revolutionize the steel-making industry with the invention of William Siemens' electric arc furnace. In 1890 Edward Allen patented the **induction furnace**. Faraday invented electro-plating – plating iron, say, with zinc to make galvanized iron sheeting, or copper spoons with silver.

In 1895 the German physicist Wilhelm Röntgen invented the **X-ray** tube. This marked the beginning of electronics – the flow of **electrons** (the tiniest bits of electricity) in gases – and the vast electronics industry.

Sewing thread filament

Thomas Alva Edison, the ▲ great American inventor, made the first really workable electric light bulb in 1879. A very fine filament of cotton thread is held by wires inside a glass bulb, from which all the air has been pumped out. When a current of electricity was passed through the wires the thread filament lit up.

THE INDUSTRIAL REVOLUTION

Revolution in Farming and Food

Food Facts

- In 1831, an American, Cyrus Hall McCormick, invented the reaper. This opened the prairies to harvesting.

- McCormick set up a farm machinery factory in Chicago. By 1856 it was turning out 4,000 machines a year.

- Margarine was invented by a French chemist, Hippolyte Mégé Mouries in 1870.

- Clarence Birdseye, an American, invented the quick freezing process in the 1920s.

- In 1939, Franklin Kidd, a British scientist, patented accelerated freeze-drying of foods.

A powerful, modern tractor, like this one, can be used for pulling a disc plough on farmland. The cabin is designed so that should the tractor roll over the driver inside is not crushed. This wheel tractor has two large rear wheels and two smaller front wheels. Some tractors have caterpillar tracks instead of wheels. ▶

Farms

As manufacturing towns grew in size so did the need for cheap food. This led to a new kind of farming – of cash crops. Farms became more mechanized with drill ploughs, horse **harrows** and seeders. Mechanized farming soon spread from England to America in the eighteenth century and then to parts of Europe. The invention of the **reaper** made it possible to harvest the rich prairie wheatlands of middle America. After the invention of the combine harvester, a **thresher** and reaper all in one, and of the tractor, farmers increased grain production.

Preserving Food

Preserving foods began in France in 1810, when Nicholas Appert, a sweet-maker, invented the process for bottling fruit. Later, canning was invented, and then, in the 1920s, the quick-freezing process. Today, some foods have chemical additives to keep them from going bad. Food is often wrapped in

Engine
Pick-up reel
Cutting bar

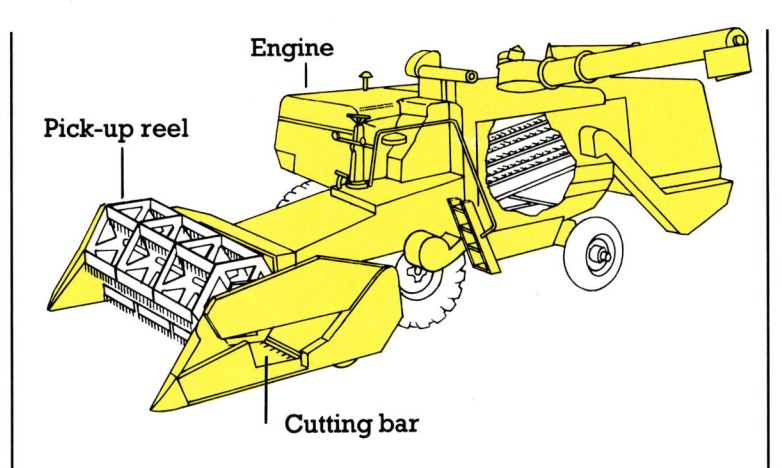

◀ The combine harvester is a combined thresher and reaper. It was widely used on the great wheat plains of North America after 1917. Smaller combines were manufactured for use on smaller farmlands. They are now used in most countries where crops are grown.

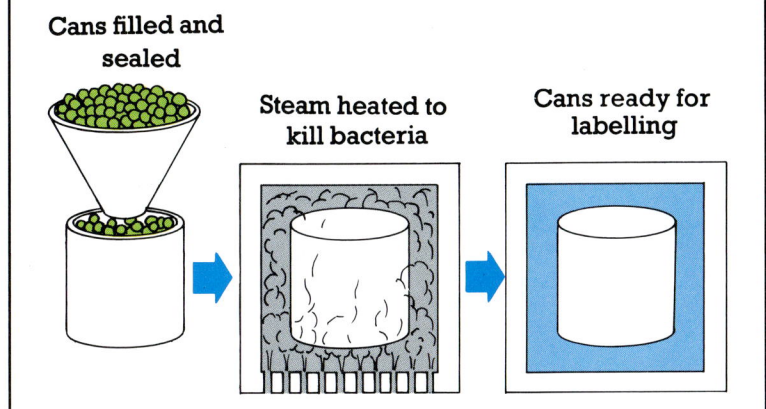

Cans filled and sealed
Steam heated to kill bacteria
Cans ready for labelling

◀ Canning is a way of preserving foods by sealing them in cans, or tins, to stop them going bad. Canning is used to preserve fruit, vegetables or meat. Tinned foods can stay fresh for a year or more. Foods are canned under very clean conditions in factories. Peter Durand, an Englishman, was the first to put food in tins in the early 1800s.

Cellophane. This was invented by Jacques Brandenburger, a Swiss chemist, in the early 1900s.

A Scientific Drink

Around 1770, Joseph Priestley, the famous chemist, dissolved carbon dioxide gas in water and found he had made a pleasant drink. It was supposed to cure scurvy, a disease suffered by sailors at the time, but it didn't. Nevertheless it has now become a steady commercial product. We know it as soda water. Priestley also discovered oxygen, ammonia, hydrogen chloride, carbon monoxide and sulphur dioxide.

Cooking with Steam

Denis Papin of France made the first pressure cooker for boiling bones for soup. He also took the first steps towards making a workable steam-engine (see page 41).

▲ Joseph Priestley (1733-1804), a British chemist, born near Leeds, in Yorkshire.

THE INDUSTRIAL REVOLUTION

Oil and Gas

From this drilling platform ▶ in the North Sea natural gas is drawn out of deep bores in the seabed. The natural gas under the seabed is usually under great pressure. When the gas field is tapped, it comes bursting up through the pipe.

Oil Facts

● James Young, a British scientist, invented a method of extracting paraffin from shale rock.

● Abraham Gesner, a Canadian chemist, invented a way to distill paraffin from crude oil.

● Edwin Drake, a retired railway guard, struck oil near Titusville, Pennsylvania, USA, in 1859. This launched the world oil industry.

An oil refinery, like this one, ▶ is an exciting sight at night. An oil refinery turns oil into petrol, diesel oil, lubricating oil and many other products.

The Oil Industry

Petroleum (literally *rock oil*) has been known since ancient times. In the Bible Noah used pitch, a kind of petroleum, to seal the seams of the Ark. The Chinese were the first to drill for oil two thousand years ago. The Egyptians greased their chariot axles with oil they found seeping from the ground. The 1850s saw inventions for extracting paraffin from shale and for distilling paraffin from oil. Paraffin was burned in lamps, heaters and stoves where no electricity was available. Farmers used paraffin in tractors.

The first purpose-built oil well was drilled in the United States in 1859 by Edwin L. Drake and launched the oil industry. In 1856 Samuel van Syckel built the first oil pipeline; it was five miles long. Today oil pipelines run thousands of miles carrying crude oil.

In 1913 the Burton **cracking** process was invented for producing petrol from oil. Many oil refineries today are pushbutton factories, entirely automated.

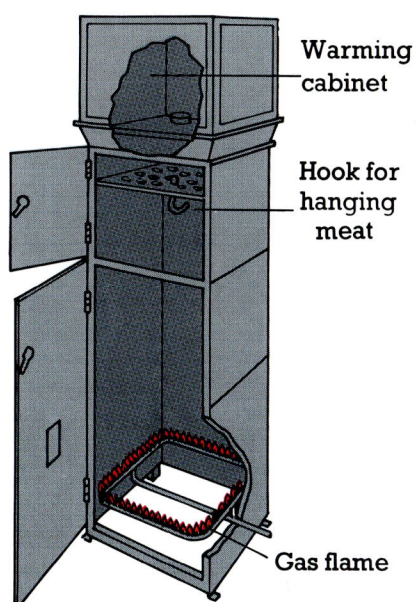

Gas cookers such as this ▲ were used in people's homes around a hundred years ago.

The Gas Industry
Most of the gas used today is natural gas, the rest is coal-gas. Today most of Britain's natural gas comes from wells in the North Sea. America also has natural gas wells.

Gas for Lighting
Up to the late 1700s, homes were lit by wax or tallow candles. Then William Murdock invented coal-gas lighting in 1792. In 1803 he lit a large factory by gaslight. In 1807 some London streets were lit. By 1850 many towns in Europe and America were using gas for street lighting and lighting homes.

Gas for Cooking
In 1832 James Sharp invented a gas stove for cooking on. In the 1840s the first gas range was built in America and in 1867 the first gas rings were in use in Britain.

Gas Facts
- Antoine Lavoisier experimented with natural gas to light city streets. In 1780 he invented a gas-holder, a huge storage tank.

- In 1813 a German businessman, Frederick Albert Winsor, formed the London and Westminster Gas Light & Coke Company, the first gas company of the world.

- In 1885 Carl Auer invented the **gas mantle**, which gave a bright white light.

- The well-known Bunsen burner of the laboratory was made popular by Robert Bunsen in the second half of the nineteenth century. It gave a steady heat by mixing air with the gas through a hole at the bottom of the burner.

7: 20th Century Technology

Mass Production

A great change in factories came in the twentieth century with the introduction of mass production. This is now giving way to automation, or production by robot machines controlled by computers.

After the American War of Independence (1773-85) Eli Whitney, inventor of the cotton gin, set up a gun-making factory. He invented a way of making guns with standardized parts, the first step towards mass production. Samuel Colt came to Whitney's factory in 1831 with a new invention, the revolver. He went on to perfect Whitney's idea in his own factory.

The Motor Car

The car has a long history. The first steam-driven car was made by a French army officer,

Here is the final assembly line at the Ford Motor Company's Highland Park factory, Detroit, in 1913. The car bodies were skidded down the wooden ramp and lowered on to the chassis as they moved along below. It was a crude start to today's mass production assembly line. ▼

CUGNOT'S TRACTION ENGINE.

Nicolas Cugnot, in 1769. Electric cars became popular in the late 1800s when Camille Faure, a French inventor, made an accumulator, a car battery that stored electricity. In 1860, in France, Etienne Lenoir built a car that ran on gas. In 1885 Gottlieb Daimler, a German engineer, patented a 'high-speed' petrol engine. He attached his engine to a bicycle, thus inventing the motorcycle. In 1886 Karl Benz built the first petrol-driven car for sale to the general public.

In 1898 the first drive shaft was fitted to a car to replace the chains that had previously linked the engine to the rear wheels. The first pneumatic (air-filled) tyres were fitted to cars in France. Then Ransom E. Olds of the United States introduced mass production methods for building cars. Cars passed along assembly lines on a trolley; the parts were fitted by semi-skilled workers. In 1908 Henry Ford perfected assembly-line manufacture and mass production in his Detroit factory. There he built his famous Model T Ford, which was remarkably cheap for its day. So was born the modern car industry.

Today's car factories are largely automated: many stages in a car's production are handled by robots controlled by computers.

▲ Nicolas Cugnot's steam traction engine, built in the 1760s, was the first true motor car. Nicolas Cugnot was a French army officer. The engine had a steam-engine, which drove a tractor. The boiler and engine hung in front of the single wheel. It was a tractor made to pull a cannon.

▲ Karl Benz, the first man to build a petrol-driven car for sale to the public.

20TH CENTURY TECHNOLOGY

Flight

Montgolfier Brothers' balloon

This picture shows three kinds of flying machine: a hot-air balloon (*left*), a biplane (*middle*) and an airship (*right*). In September 1783, the Montgolfier brothers rose in their hot-air balloon in front of King Louis XVI of France. They had with them a lamb, a duck and a cockerel. Early biplanes had two wings and fixed wheels for landing. *La France*, was the first successful airship. It could go at 14 mph!

People have always dreamed of flying. The first ascent was made by the French Montgolfier brothers in a balloon in 1783. In 1785 J. B. Meusnier designed a propeller-driven aircraft, but his idea was ignored. In 1804 Sir George Cayley invented a glider. Arthur Renard and Charles Krebs built the first steam-powered airship, *La France*, in 1884. The Wright brothers flew the first powered, heavier-than-air machine in 1903. They had to invent all the parts of their flying machine including propellers, wing flaps and rudder. They even had to build their own petrol engine: car companies were suspicious of letting them use a car engine in case flying hurt the car business! In the 1920s aeroplanes began to be made of metal. In the 1930s single-winged monoplanes replaced double-winged biplanes.

The Jet and Space Age

Jet aeroplanes are powered by jet engines. They do not use propellers. They raised the speed record incredibly high. The first jet propulsion engine was patented by Group Captain Frank Whittle of the Royal Air Force in

A biplane

La France

1930. The first supersonic (faster-than-sound) flight was made in 1947 over America in the rocket-powered Bell X-1 flown by Chuck Yeager. It broke the **sound barrier** now broken daily by Concorde. Aeroplanes began to carry much heavier loads, with the arrival of passenger-carrying aircraft. In 1953 the first passenger helicopter service was opened. Helicopters are now a familiar sight. In 1954 the inventor Barnes Wallis designed the VTOL (vertical take-off and landing) aircraft, with pivoting engines.

In 1926 Robert H. Goddard built the first liquid-fuelled rocket. In 1957 the USSR launched the first satellite, Sputnik I. The USSR also put the first man into space, Major Yuri Gagarin, in 1961. In 1969 Neil Armstrong became the first man to walk on the moon. The USSR is planning to land a man on the planet Mars in a few years time.

A space shuttle is launched ▲ from the Kennedy Space Center, Florida, USA. It is taking astronauts John Young and Robert Crippen into orbit.

◄ This is the Bell X-1 rocket plane. It made the world's first supersonic flight on 14 October 1947.

55

20TH CENTURY TECHNOLOGY

Getting the Message Across

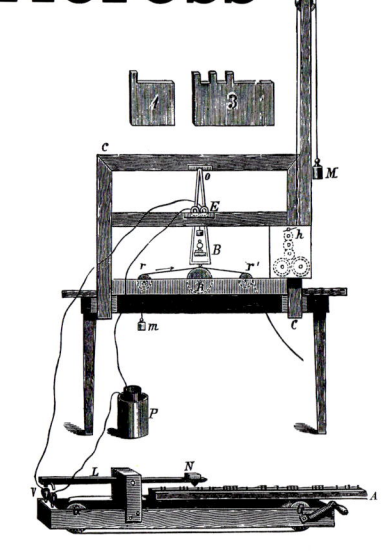

Modern communications began with Samuel Morse's invention of electric telegraphy in 1840. In 1878 Thomas Edison invented the phonograph, or gramophone, out of which grew the giant record industry of records, cassettes and compact discs.

In 1876 Alexander Graham Bell invented the telephone. By 1900 half the American people were within reach of a telephone.

In 1895 Guglielmo Marconi invented the radio, which, by the 1920s, became common in people's homes. The BBC opened the world's first television service in Britain in 1936.

The Cinema

In 1826 a Frenchman, Joseph Nicéphore Niepce, took the first photograph, of the courtyard of his house. In 1839 an Englishman, William Fox Talbot, made the first photograph from a **negative**. In 1947 Edwin H. Land invented the Polaroid Land camera, which develops photographs in 60 seconds.

The first moving pictures were made in the 1890s by a number of inventors: Thomas Edison, George Eastman and William Friese-Greene. The cinema business began when the Lumière brothers projected silent moving pictures on a screen for a paying audience in Paris in 1895. In 1927 the first successful talking film was made.

The picture shows a sketch ▲ of Samuel Morse's first model of his invention, the electric telegraph. At the bottom is a notched rod, called a *port rule*. This operates the key of this telegraph-sending device. It sent out messages as a series of dots and dashes along electric wires.

This picture shows a ▶ communications satellite in orbit round the Earth. It was taken from the space shuttle Discovery. Communications satellites transmit messages from one part of the Earth to another.

56

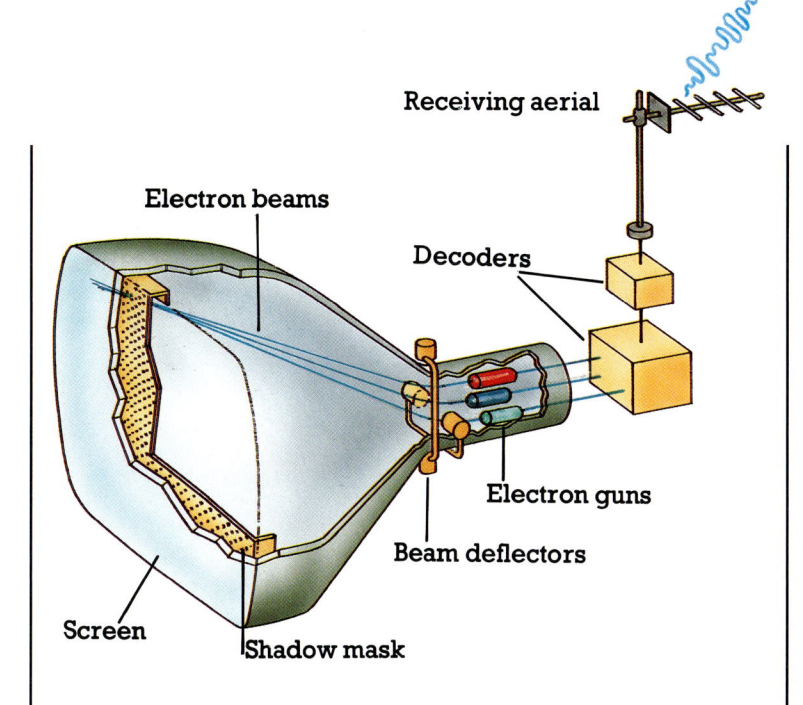

◀ The television aerial picks up the signals from the television station, and they go on to the decoders. These send the signal down into the three electron guns. Each gun shoots a beam of electrons at the screen. The shadow mask behind the screen guides the beams to strike coloured phosphor dots of red, green and blue on the screen.

Television

Television grew out of two inventions: the photo-electric cell and the Crookes tube. The photo-cell turns light into electric current. The Crookes tube, an early X-ray tube, is coated on the inside so it gives off light when struck by electrons: this is the basis of the television tube. Many inventors worked through the 1920s and 30s to produce television. After World War II, television took off in Europe, the United States and Japan. Colour television began in the United States in 1953. In 1962 the first television pictures were transmitted from the United States to Europe via **satellite**. In 1965 an American space probe sent back television pictures to Earth from Mars.

Communications Facts

● The first words Alexander Graham Bell spoke into his newly-invented telephone were 'Mr Watson, come here! I want you!'

● The first words Thomas Edison recorded on his phonograph, or talking machine, were 'Mary had a little lamb.'

● The first gramophone used a wooden needle. Now compact discs are 'read' by **laser** beams. Lasers were invented in the 1960s.

● In 1817, the Swedish chemist Baron Jons Berzelius invented the photo-cell. It turned light signals into electric current.

● Three main inventors worked on the invention of television: an American, Philo T. Farnsworth, a Scotsman, John Logie Baird, and a Russian, Vladimir Zworikyn.

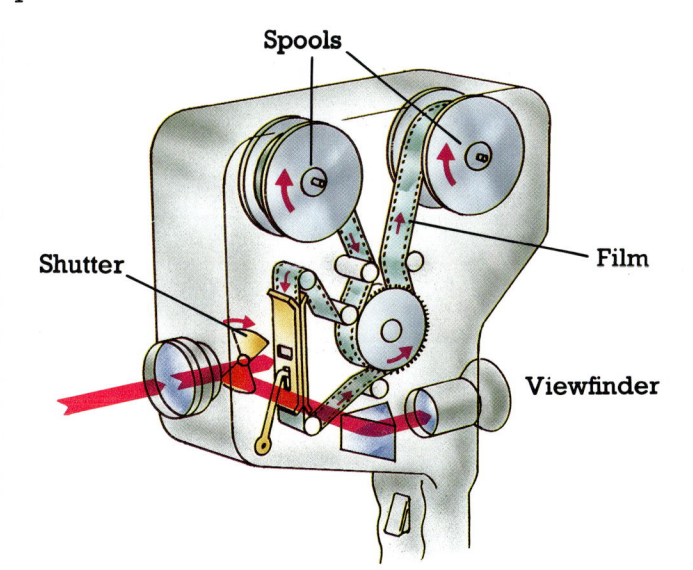

◀ A movie camera takes photos in the same way as a still camera does. The film is divided up into frames; the shutter stops the film for a fraction of a second while the light passes through the lens and the picture is taken on the frame. Then the next frame moves into position. The exposed film is wound on to the back spool.

20TH CENTURY TECHNOLOGY

The Computer and the Future

This is a sketch of Charles ▶ Babbage's first computer. As numbers were fed into the right-hand column, they turned cogs that after ten turns turned a cog in the next column to the left by one notch. And so on.

The picture shows a ▲ laboratory where computers are developed. Here the computers of the future are designed and improved.

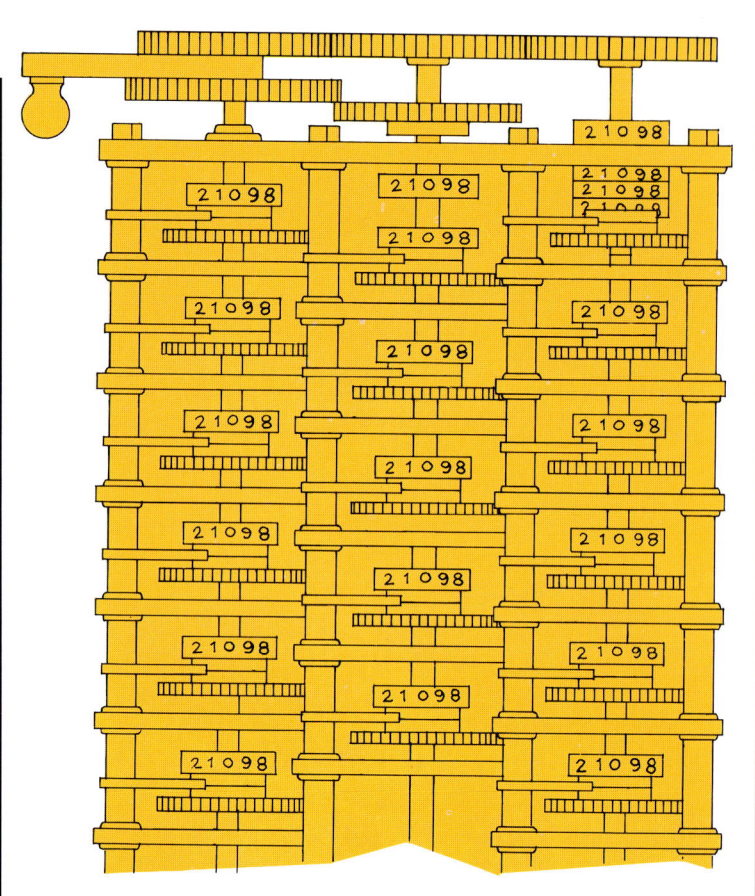

Little did Charles Babbage realize what he was starting when he began work on his calculating engine in 1832. He never finished his machine but all the ideas were right. The first electronic computer was built in America in 1945. In 1947 the **transistor** was invented. This made it possible to reduce computers from the size of a room to that of a typewriter! Space research led the way to even smaller computers. Computers now control airport traffic, road traffic lights, nuclear power stations, complete car factories and coal-mines. Future computers will be designed by computers. Computers can now be programmed to recognize the human voice and can translate from one language into another; they can even read typescript.

The kitchen of the future may be pre-programmed like a washing machine to cook without the help of humans, whether by microwave oven or by conventional sources of heat, such as electricity or gas. Food will be processed entirely in computer-run factories.

New ways of storing information include magnetic tape, **floppy discs**, compact discs and the hologram. A hologram is really a flat negative, like a photo negative; when lights are shone through it, it creates a three-dimensional picture.

Tomorrow's Inventor

The days of the gifted amateur inventor are numbered. The age of the inventor with a smattering of science ended with Thomas Edison. His work in electricity, telegraphy, moving pictures and sound recording helped lay the foundations of the modern electrical and electronics industries. Computers and much else will be designed by computers themselves in the future. No longer will inventors work in lonely garrets or cellars. Tomorrow's inventors will work as part of a team in well-equipped laboratories. They will be paid whether they get results or not. Perhaps computers will be the inventors of tomorrow.

▲ This picture shows an artist's impression of what a space station of the future may look like. It will orbit in space far above the Earth.

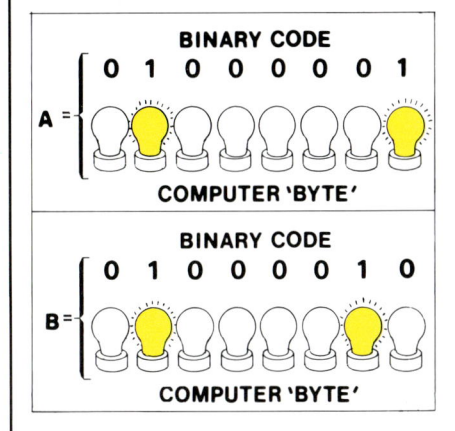

▲ Computers basically work by a series of on/off switches which represent *binary* numbers. Binary numbers are made up only of 1s and 0s. The numbers shown here are 65 and 66. Each piece of information like this in the computer is called a byte.

Glossary

Alchemist: A kind of chemist in the Middle Ages. He tried to turn base metals, like lead, into gold and silver in his laboratory.
Alloy: A mixture of metals. Brass is an alloy of copper and zinc.
Arch: A curved structure, usually to support weight above an opening.
Astronomy: The science of the stars and planets and other bodies in the sky.
Axle: A spindle about which a wheel turns.
Babylon: A great capital city in ancient Mesopotamia.
Backers: People who back a project, that is, they put money into it.
Ballistics: The science of the motion of bodies hurled through the air, such as bullets and cannon balls.
Barometer: An instrument used to measure the pressure of the atmosphere (air).
Battering ram: A war machine used in ancient and medieval times to smash open gaps in the walls or gates of castles or town walls.
Block and tackle: A pulley or system of pulleys used to lift heavy loads.
Bolas: Two or three strings, with wooden balls at each end, tied together. Herdsmen whirl them around and throw them to wind round the legs of cattle so they can catch them.
Charcoal: A form of carbon made by burning animal or vegetable substances in little air.
Compass card: This shows the sixteen points of the compass, North, South, East, West, North north-east, North-east, East north-east etc.
Counterweight: A weight that balances another weight.
Cracking: A way of applying heat and pressure to break down oil into its lighter components such as petrol.
Cretans: People who lived in ancient Crete, an island in the Mediterranean Sea.
Cross staff: An instrument for finding the angle of the sun above the horizon at sea. It was used in the Renaissance.
Depression: A period when the economy fails, prices fall and many workers are unemployed. The Great Depression of the 1920s is an example of this.
Domesday Book: The first record of the lands of England with their ownership, extent and value. It was made by William the Conqueror in 1086.
Dug-out: A canoe dug out of a log.
Electromagnetic waves: Waves of electrical and magnetic energy, such as radio waves, light waves, ultra-violet waves, and X-rays.
Electrons: Tiny centres of electric charge that circle the core of an atom.
Fax: A kind of copying machine that sends copies of pictures or letters from one telephone to another.
Fire damp: The miners' name for an explosive mixture of methane and air that forms in coal-mines.
Floppy disc: A plastic disc (not actually 'floppy') that is placed in a computer. It stores the programs that drive the computer.
Force pump: A simple pump with some form of motor that forces water through pipes.
Friction: The stickiness or roughness that stops objects moving freely when they are moved across one another. It is a rubbing effect.
Gas mantle: A lace-like hood placed over a gas jet. It is made of a heat-resisting material that glows white hot in the burning gas flame and gives out light.
Geometry: The branch of mathematics that deals with the measurement of space: points, lines, surfaces and solids.
Harness: The leather gear of a draught horse or ox. It usually consists of a bridle, reins, blinkers, collar, girth and so on.
Harrow: Used by a farmer to break up the clods of earth into finer bits before sowing seed. It can be a disc harrow or a drag harrow.
Hemisphere: A half a sphere or globe. The two halves fitted together make the whole sphere again.
Hinge: A movable joint, usually of metal, like that hung on the side post of a door. The door swings open on the hinge.
Hypodermic: A fine, hollow needle for injecting medical drugs under a patient's skin. Hypodermic means 'under the skin'.
Inclined plane: A slope or ramp, used for rolling things up and down.
Induction furnace: A kind of furnace to melt metals. An alternating current is made to go through the metal, which heats it up.
Irrigation: The watering of soil and crops by artificial means. Water from wells or rivers is channelled into ditches to irrigate the land.
Keel: A flat piece of metal or wood fixed to the hull (bottom) of a boat that extends into the water to stop it tipping over.
Laboratory: A room or building where scientific tests, experiments, and so on are carried out.
Laser: A device that produces an extremely intense, narrow beam of light.
Lathe: A machine-tool for shaping, boring and cutting metal or wood.
Lever: A bar used to prise up a heavy object.

A see-saw is a simple lever.
Lyre: A stringed musical instrument used by the Greeks and Egyptians.
Magnetite: Iron oxide that is magnetic. The first magnetite was called lodestone.
Mayans: Indians who developed a remarkable civilization in Central America between AD 600 and 900. They built strange stepped pyramids.
Mesopotamia: The land between the Tigris and the Euphrates rivers in what is now Iraq. The rivers run into the Persian Gulf.
Meteorites: Chunks of stone or iron that strike the Earth from outer space.
Microbes: Extremely small living creatures.
Middle Ages: Lasted from about AD 480 to the late 1400s in Europe. Also known as the medieval period.
Navigation: The science of finding your way from one place to another. It is a method of finding the position of a ship, aeroplane, etc. by scientific instruments.
Negative: A photographic image in which light and dark are reversed or colours replaced by complementary ones.
Nocturnal: An instrument used by navigators in the Middle Ages for finding the time at night by 'shooting the stars'.
Organism: Any living plant or animal.
Original: The earliest example of a thing or something entirely new.
Pendulum: In its simplest form, a small weight hanging and swinging from a supported string. Old clocks have pendulums.
Philosopher: A person who thinks about questions such as 'What is good?', 'What is freedom?' and so on. Many philosophers work in universities.
Phoenicians: Peoples who lived about 2000 BC in the Eastern Mediterranean lands. They developed navigation, sailing and trade.
Pig iron: Iron made in blast-furnaces, so called because some of it is cast into bars called 'pigs'.
Protractor: A mathematical instrument for measuring angles.
Pulley: A fixed wheel over which a rope or chain is passed for lifting or hoisting up heavy loads.
Reaper: A reaping machine used by farmers for harvesting grain. Reapers are used for cutting corn in North America and Australia.
Renaissance: A time in European history between about 1420 and about 1520 that saw a revival in interest in art and science.
Satellite: Something that orbits round a planet, like the Moon round the Earth. Artificial satellites are launched from the Earth.
Semites: A group of peoples who spoke Semitic, an early Middle East language. They included Assyrians, Hebrews, Carthaginians and Phoenicians.
Sickle: A curved tool for cutting corn, used by farmers. It is like a small scythe.
Sound barrier: A build-up of air pressure as an aeroplane approaches the speed of sound. When the aeroplane 'breaks the sound barrier' there is a loud sonic boom.
Spokes: A set of rods or bars that radiate out from the hub of a wheel to its rim.
Stern post: A flat kind of rudder fixed to the high, flat sterns of Chinese junks.
Stirrup: An iron loop with a flattened base hanging by a strap from a saddle for a horse-rider to put his foot in.
Sumerians: A people who lived in Sumer, Mesopotamia, about 3000 BC.
Symbol: A sign, like a letter of the alphabet, that stands for an idea or a sound.
Tar macadam: A tarry stuff for road surfaces, made of tiny stones and tar or asphalt.
Thresher: A piece of farm machinery that combines four operations: threshing, separating, cleaning and stacking the cut corn.
Token: A sign, symbol or mark. Token money was once used. The coin had no value in itself, only what it stood for.
Transistor: A small electronic device used in computers, radios and TV sets. It controls the flow of electrons like a valve.
Treadmill: A large, wide wheel that turns, with steps round the rim. Treadmills were worked by horses or humans in olden times.
Trip hammer: A high-speed, power-driven hammer used to shape small forgings such as tool or machine parts.
Vacuum: Empty space. A vacuum flask for keeping liquids hot has a vacuum between its glass double walls.
Wireless telegraphy: A way of sending messages by radio through the air. The telegraph messages are made up of Morse code – dots and dashes.
Word processor: A computerized typewriter that stores all the words typed in its memory.
Wrought iron: Iron containing tiny, glassy threads of iron silicate. It resists corrosion.
X-rays: A type of electromagnetic wave. You cannot see them. They are used by doctors and dentists to see 'inside' the body.
Yarns: Fibres of wool, silk, cotton or flax, spun for use in weaving and knitting.
Yoke: A curved piece of wood over horses' and oxen's necks fastened to a plough or cart that the animal pulls along.

Index

A **Bold** number shows the entry is illustrated on that page. The same page often has writing about the entry too.

abacus **15**
accumulator (storage battery) 53
aeroplanes **6**, 54-5
agriculture 10, **11**, 19, 48-9, 58
   see also irrigation
air pressure **7**, 8, **36-7**
airships 54, **55**
alphabets **14**, 15
Anachasis (Greek inventor) 20
ancient world, cities of the 16-17, **19**
Appert, Nicholas (French sweet-maker) 48
aqueducts 16, **17**
arches 16, **17**
Archimedes (Greek inventor) 16
Arkwright, Richard (British inventor) 42
armour **24**
Armstrong, Neil (American astronaut) 55
assembly lines **52**, 53
astrolabes **22**
Auer, Carl 51
axles 12, **13**

Babbage, Charles (British inventor) 58
Baird, John Logie (Scottish inventor) 57
ballistics **27**
balloons, hot air **54**
barometers 36, **37**
battering 10
batteries, electric 46, 53
battering rams 24
Bell, Alexander Graham (American inventor) 6-**7**, 56, 57
Bell X-1 (supersonic plane) **55**
Benz, Karl (German inventor) **53**
Berzelius, Baron Jons (Swiss chemist) 57
Bessemer, Henry (British inventor) 44-5
bicycles **8**
binary code **59**
biplanes 54, **55**
Birdseye, Clarence (American inventor) 48
biremes (Phoenician ships) 20
blacksmiths **18**

blast-furnaces **45**
Brandenburger, Jacques (Swiss chemist) 48-9
Bunsen, Robert (German chemist) 51

'calculating engine', Babbage's **58**
calculators 36, 58
cannons **26**, 27
cars 4, **52**-3
Cartwright, Edmund (British clergyman) 43
catapults **24-5**
Cayley, Sir George (British inventor) 54
chariots 24, **25**
chronometers 23, **33**
cinema 5, 56
cities of the ancient world 16-17, **19**
clepsydra (clock) **17**
Clermont (steamship) 41
clocks 5, **17**, 28, **32**, **33**
clotenbrots 28
coal-mining and engines **38**, 39
Cockerell, C. S. (British inventor) 7
cogs 13, **34**, **35**
Colt, Samuel (American inventor) 52
combine harvesters **49**
communication, electronic 5, 56-7
compact discs 56, 57
compass, magnetic 22, **23**
computers, 5, **58**, **59**
cookers 5, 10, **49**, 58
Cort, Henry (British inventor) 44
cotton gins and mules **42**
Crippen, Robert (American astronaut) 55
Crompton, Samuel (British inventor) 42
Crookes tube (television) 56
cross staffs 23
Cugnot, Nicolas 52-3
curettes (surgeon's knives) 17

Daimler, Gottlieb (German engineer) 53
Darby, Abraham (British inventor) 44
Darrow, Charles B. (American inventor) 8
Davy, Sir Humphrey (British inventor) 38, 39
Drake, Edwin L. 50

Dunlop, John (British inventor) 8
Durand, Peter (British inventor) 49

Eastman, George 56
Edison, Thomas Alva (American inventor) 6, 47 56, 57
electricity, the age of **5**, 6, 7, 46-7, 58
electromagnetic waves 6-7
   see also radio, television
electronics 5, 47, 56-7
Ericsson, John (British inventor) 41
explosives 26, 27
eye-glasses **30**, 31

Fahrenheit, Gabriel Daniel (German inventor) 36
Faraday, Michael (British inventor) 6, 46-**7**
farming 10, **11**, 19, 48-9, 58
   see also irrigation
Farnsworth, Philo T. (American inventor) 57
Faure, Camille (French inventor) 53
fax [facsimile] machines 5
Ferris, George (British inventor) 8
Fertile Crescent 19
fire, using 10-11
Fitch, John (American inventor) 41
flight **6**, 28, **29**, 54-5
Flyer, the (Wright brothers' plane) 6
food-processing 48-**9**, 58
Ford, Henry (American car maker) 52, 53
La France (airship) 54, **55**
Franklin, Benjamin (American inventor) 46
Friese-Green, William 56
Fulton, Robert 41
furnaces 44, **45**, 47

Gagarin, Major Yuri (Russian cosmonaut) 55
Galileo (Italian inventor) 30, **32**, 36
galleys, Greek and Roman 20
gas **5**, **51**, 58
gears 13, **34**, **35**
Gesner, Abraham 50
Gillette, King (American inventor) 9

Goddard, Robert H. 55
Godfrey, Thomas (American inventor) 23
gramophones 6, 56, 57
Guericke, Otto von (German inventor) 37
gunpowder and guns **26**-7, 28, 52
Gutenberg, Johannes 36, **37**

Hadley, John (British inventor) 23
Hargreaves, James (British inventor) 42
Harrison, John (British inventor) 33
Hartman, George (German inventor) 22
helicopters 29, 55
Henry, Joseph (American inventor) 6
hieroglyphs 14, **15**
Hipparchus (Greek inventor) 22
Hooke, Robert (British scientist) 33
hour-glass **32**
hovercraft **7**
Hunt, Walter (American inventor) 6
hunting **10**, 11
Huygens, Christian (Dutch inventor) 32-3
hypodermic needles 7

Industrial Revolution 38-51
inventors 6-7
  see also by name
iron-making **44**, 45
irrigation **13**, **16**, **17**, **34**, **35**

Janssen, Zacharias 31
jet planes 54, **55**

Keller, Friedrich Gottlieb (German inventor) 15
Kidd, Franklin (British scientist) 48
Kleist, E. J. von 46
Krebs, Charles (French inventor) 54

Land, Edward H. (American photographer) 56
Lavoisier, Antoine 51
Lawson, H. J. (British inventor) 8
Leeuwenhoek, Antony van **31**
Lenoir, Etienne (French inventor) 53
lenses *see* microscopes, telescopes
Leonardo da Vinci 28-**9**
levers **4**, 12, 16, **17**
  see also catapults, slings
light bulbs 6, **47**
lodestones (early compasses) 22
long boats, Viking 20, **21**
Lumiére brothers (French inventors) 56

McCormick, Cyrus Hall (American inventor) 48
Magdeburg hemispheres **36**-**7**
magnification *see* microscopes, telescopes
maps **21**
Marconi, Guglielmo (Italian inventor) 6-7, **9**, 56
mass production 44, 52-3
mathematics 14, 15, 16, 29
Maxim, Hiram (US-British inventor) 7
Mestral, Georges de (Swiss inventor) 9
metal revolution, the 44-5
microscopes 30, **31**
'Miner's Friend', the **39**
miner's safety lamp **38**, 39
Model-T Ford **52**, 53
money 4, 10-11
Montgolfier brothers **54**
Morse, Samuel (American inventor) 56
Mouries, Hippolyte Mégé (French chemist) 48
movie camera **57**
Murdock, William (British inventor) 51
Musschenbroek, Pieter von (Dutch inventor) 46

navigation **21**, 22-3, **33**
Newcomen, Thomas (British inventor) 39
Nicéphore, Joseph (French photographer) 56
nocturnals 23
numbers, invention of 14, 15

oil and gas 50-1
Olds, Ransom E. (American car maker) 53

paddle-wheel boats **41**
paper-making 15
Papin, Denis (French inventor) 41, 49
paraffin 50

Pascal, Blaise (French mathematician) 36
Pasteur, Louis (French scientist) 31
patents and sales 8-9
Penny Farthing **8**
petroleum 50, 53
phonographs 6, 56
photography 56, **57**
Pi Sheng (Chinese printer) 36
pistons, double-action **40**
Polaroid Land camera 56
power looms **43**
Pravaz, Charles Gabriel (French inventor) 7
Priestley, Joseph (British chemist) **49**
production lines **52**, 53
'Puffing Billy' 40, **41**
pulleys 16, **17**
pumps 16, 29, 37
  see also irrigation
pyramids 12, 16

radio 5, 6-7, **9**
railway locomotives 40, **41**
razor blades 8
reapers 48, **49**
Réaumur, René de (French inventor) 44
rebus (picture) puzzles 14
record players 6, 56
refinery, oil **50**
Renard, Arthur (French inventor) 54
river boats **19**, 20
Robert, Louis Nicolas (French inventor) 15
Rocket, Stephenson's 40, **41**
rockets **55**
rocking beam engine **39**
Röntgen, Wilhelm (German physicist) 47
rope stretchers, Egyptian 16
Rosetta Stone, the **15**
rudders 20

sails **19**
sand-timers **32**
satellites, communication **56**, 57
Savannah (steamship) 41
Savery, Captain Thomas (British inventor) 39
scaling ladders 24
screw, Archimedes' **16**
see-saws **4**
Seely, Henry (American inventor) 7
sextants **22**-**3**

shaduf **17**
Sharp, James (American inventor) 51
ships 9, 18-23
   early transport 18-19
   finding the way 22-3
   sailing 20-1
   steam **41**
siege machines **24-5**
Siemens, William (German inventor) 45, 47
Slater, Samuel (British inventor) 43
slings and sling-shots **24-5**
space age, the 54-5
space shuttle **55**
spectacles **30**, 31
spinning industry, the **42**, **43**
spring traps **10**
Sputnik I (Russian satellite) 55
static electricity **46**
steam, the age of 5, **39**, **40**, **41**
steam-engine 5, 39, 40, 41
steel-making **44**, **45**
Stephenson, George (British inventor) 40, 41
submarines 28
sundials **32**
Swinton, Ernest (British inventor) 6
Syckel, Samuel van 50

Talbot, William Fox (British photographer) 56
technology, modern 47, 52-9
telegraphy 9, **56**
telephones 5, 56
telescopes **30**
television **5**, 6, 56, **57**
textiles *see* spinning industry
Thomas, Gilchrist (British inventor) 45
Thomson, R. W. (British inventor) 8
threshers 48, **49**
time, telling the 5, **17**, 28, **32**, **33**
token goods **11**
tools, making 10-11
Torricelli, Evangelista (Italian inventor) 36
tractors **48**
transport, early 18-19
travois (horse-drawn pack sled) **12**
trebuchets (Chinese sling-shot machines) 25
Trevithick, Richard (British inventor) 40, 41

Ts'ai Lun (Chinese inventor) 15
tyres, air-filled 8, 53

vacuum pumps 37
   see also light bulbs
Vecro fasteners **9**
Vitruvius (Roman engineer) 24
Volta, Alessandro (Italian inventor) **46**
VTOL (Vertical Take-Off and Landing) aircraft 55

Wallis, Barnes (British inventor) 55
war, 6, 7, 16, 24-7, 28
   gunpowder and cannons 26-7, **53**
   slings and catapults 24-5
water-mills **34**, 35
water-wheels 13
Watt, James (British inventor) 5, 40, 44
wheels, 12-**13**
Whitney, Eli (American inventor) 43, 52
Whittle, Frank (British inventor) 54-5
windmills 34-**5**
Winsor, Frederick Albert 51
word processors **5**
words and numbers 5, 14-15
Wright brothers (American inventors) **6**, 54

X-ray tubes 47

Yaeger, Chuck (American pilot) 55
yokes **12**
Young, James (British scientist) 50
Young, John (American astronaut) 55

Zworikyn, Vladimir (Russian inventor) 57